A Blade of Grass:
New Palestinian Poetry

A Blade of Grass:
New Palestinian Poetry

edited by Naomi Foyle

Smokestack Books
1 Lake Terrace, Grewelthorpe, Ripon HG4 3BU
e-mail: info@smokestack-books.co.uk
www.smokestack-books.co.uk

ISBN 978-0-9957675-3-9

Smokestack Books
is represented
by Inpress Ltd

Contents

Introduction

'Against barbarity, poetry must stand with human
frailty, like a blade of grass in a wall as armies march
by.'

Mahmoud Darwish (1941-2008)

A Blade of Grass is only the second compilation of Palestinian
poetry to be published in the UK. Like its sister volume, the land-
mark multilingual Scottish-Palestinian anthology *A Bird is Not a
Stone*, it represents a small step on the road to the long-overdue
recognition Palestinian poetry deserves in the Anglophone world.
Aiming to reflect the Palestinian experience in all its contemporary
dimensions, it showcases new work from a wide variety of poets:
new and established voices from the Palestinian territories, the
diaspora, and from within the disputed borders of Israel; women
and men writing in a diverse set of forms and on a broad range of
themes – expected and necessary, surprising and challenging. It
includes bilingual poets who translate their own work and
Palestinian poets who write in English. The result of a dialogue
with poets and translators across languages and cultures, in falafel
shops, emails, smartphones and conducted in Skype calls, this
book is a kind of microcosm of global Palestinian poetic activity
in Arabic and English, reflecting the dynamic pluralism of that
endeavour, and yet also just scratching its surface.

In their steadfast witnessing of the Palestinian catastrophe over
the decades, Palestinian poets have created a body of work that
addresses with relentless creativity the most searching question art
asks of us all: how to transform human suffering into personal and
collective growth. But beyond that, as human ecologist Andreas
Malm trenchantly argues, in asserting the survival of the
Palestinian people and honouring their yearning to return to their
land, Palestinian writers have anticipated and plumbed the great
themes of the twenty-first century. For everywhere the line
between refugee and resident is muddying: the increasing threats
of severe weather events, environmental degradation and nuclear
war are creating a volatile and insecure world for even the wealthy.
Malm cites Naomi Klein, from her 2016 Edward Said lecture:

> The state of longing for a radically altered homeland – a home
> that may not even exist any longer – is something that is being
> rapidly, and tragically, globalised... If we don't demand radical
> change we are headed for a whole world of people searching for
> a home that no longer exists.

Palestinian poets, then, are the voices of our mutual future. But though climate change may yet unite humanity in a call to transform our bankrupt global economic order, given the distinct, severe and complex pressures under which Palestinian poets live and write, their work does not permit easy identifications.

To complicate matters further, translation is a double-edged blade that can cut against its own best intentions. In his introduction to his translation of *The Silence That Remains* by Ghassan Zaqtan, Fady Joudah quotes Jean Genet's claim that translation answers a human need to experience 'the ecstasy of betrayal'. In a colonial context, where Palestinian poets are celebrated even as their cultural and political annihilation accelerates, this remains a disturbing insight. But translation is also a crucial, loving attempt at communication. This book's title is a small example of the creative conversation that translation can enact.[1] The image of a blade of grass carries paradoxical connotations: a tender green knife, incapable of drawing blood, yet which expresses a power greater than that of any army's. Like 'sheep', however, the Arabic term for grass takes identical singular and plural forms. The Arabic title of this book, *Shafra min al-'ushb* ['blade/knife of grass'] is therefore, according to my Palestinian friend Rewa' Attieh: 'really strange – but not violent at all . . . something like poetry'. Yet that small jolt tells a sharper truth. Against the attempted erasure of Palestine from the world map, translation is also a weapon in the long, slow Palestinian revolution.

The word is not lightly used. To achieve a just peace in Israel/Palestine will take nothing short of a revolution: for all the current and rightful inhabitants of the region, Jews and Arabs, to equitably share the land, the political status quo will have to change dramatically, with Israel not only acknowledging the UN mandated Right of Return for all Palestinian refugees, but addressing the core contradiction between being a Jewish and a democratic state. Although such a radical transformation may seem impossible, the Palestinian experience has taught us that revolution is not an event, or even a process, but a state of mind: an electric commitment to human dignity, justice, and solidarity, charged by an uncompromising vision of freedom. Like their brothers and sisters in South Africa, another place where the impossible needed to happen, and did, Palestinians have had an excruciatingly long time to develop and hone this elevated consciousness.

This book is published one hundred years less a day after the Balfour Declaration, that wrongful promise of the British government, made on 2 November 1917, to support the establishment of a national Jewish homeland in land already occupied by other peoples. This insurmountable difficulty was clear to the early Zionists: as Palestinian historian and memoirist Ghada Karmi reports in a book that takes its title from the encounter, two Viennese Rabbis on a fact-finding mission in 1897 warned their circle back home that 'the bride is beautiful, but she is married to another man'. The obstacle, however, was deemed a mere inconvenience. In 1948 the state of Israel was created, in a war that destroyed over five hundred Palestinian villages, dislocated over 750,000 people, and claimed far more land than the UN had granted the new country. This expansionist settler-colonial project has continued unabated until, today, the descendants of those evicted Palestinians number approximately six and half million refugees, nearly four million of them living in UN camps as the world's forgotten people, while Gaza has been under siege for ten years, its economy stifled and its hospitals, schools, farms, electricity plants and people, down to its many children, periodically subject to ruthless bombardment. In the West Bank and Jerusalem, decades of land grabs have corroded any hope of a viable Palestinian state, while travel restrictions, checkpoints and erratic access to basic services make daily life a constant battle against humiliation, frustration, fear, anger and despair.

Inevitably, the conflict has generated cycles of violence, but the mainstream media fixation on rockets and knife attacks obscures the fact that, as eco-scientist and human rights activist Mazin Qumsiyeh has extensively documented, since the times of Ottoman Rule, Palestinian civil society has overwhelmingly responded to occupation, ethnic cleansing and injustice with *muqawama sha'biyya*, or popular resistance, large swathes of people engaging in forms of mass peaceful protest. This year alone, a prisoners' hunger strike won the right of family visits and the al-Aqsa mosque protests, in which thousands of people prayed and demonstrated on the streets of Jerusalem, forced the Israeli government to remove the metal detectors it had installed at one of Islam's holiest sites. These victories come after a decade of flourishing popular resistance, including the Open Bethlehem campaign, Qumsiyeh's Palestine Museum of Biodiversity, and, most visibly of all, the international Boycott Divestment and Sanctions (BDS) movement, which for ten years now has been steadily building support for its inclusive demand for a human rights-based future for Israel/Palestine. Israeli historian Ilan Pappé observed in 2015 that Palestinian activists are writing a 'new dictionary' of resistance, in which the terms 'ethnic cleansing', 'apartheid', 'decolonisation' and 'one state solution' replace the moribund shibboleths of the 'two state solution' and 'peace process', with their false assumption of parity between the two parties. For although there is violence on both sides of the conflict, only one side has tanks, fighter jets and nuclear weapons, only one has a financial umbilical cord to the United States treasury, and only one is an occupying force, violating international law on an industrial scale.

Inseparable from all this activity is the sense of a burgeoning, internationally recognised Palestinian cultural resistance. With its call for cultural and academic boycott the BDS movement has made culture itself a double-edged grass blade, focusing the world's attention not only on Israel's restrictions on freedom of speech, but also on Palestinian creative expression. Cultural resistance in this latter sense has three main dimensions. Through their art, literature, music, dance, cuisine and national dress, Palestinians affirm their identity and survival; creatively develop their revolutionary consciousness; and, in their claim on a world audience, significantly address the huge narratological disparity in the conflict. The Zionist narrative, forged as it is from a long traumatic history of persecution culminating in the crime against humanity that was the Holocaust, is embedded like shrapnel in the post-war Euro-

American psyche; the Palestinian story, though, is barely known in the West, their catastrophe, the Nakba of 1948, reduced to the odd sepia photo of refugee columns, the anniversary eclipsed by Israeli Independence Day, while in Israel itself, Nakba commemoration is a criminal offense. This distorted view of the conflict, in which Israel is always portrayed as the victim, justifies and perpetuates Zionist state atrocities, and redressing the imbalance is a crucial prerequisite to establishing a just peace in the region.

Palestinian cultural resistance is doing that work, and in its multiplicity, vitality and determination is building an unstoppable momentum. Like BDS, roaming literary festival Palfest celebrated its tenth anniversary in 2017, while The Freedom Theatre in Jenin refugee camp having survived the 2011 assassination of its charismatic co-founder, Juliano Mer Khamis, marked its eleventh year with tours of America, India and the UK. Also over this period, visual artists including Samia Halaby, Leila Shawa, Larissa Sansour and this book's cover artist, Belal Khaled, have achieved or consolidated international renown, Palestinian prose writers including Raja Shehadeh, Selma Dabbagh, Susan Abulhawa and Mischa Hiller have emerged to acclaim, and Bashir Abu-Manneh has published the first English-language study of the Palestinian novel. Pop culture has not gone untouched either: thrillingly for young people in the region, two Palestinian singers in the last four years have won Arab Idol.

More than any other art form, however, the Palestinian cultural resistance has been defined by poetry and poets, most famously Darwish, whose inexhaustible body of work honours every fragile stem of the grassroots, and whose readings famously drew audiences of tens of thousands of people from all walks of life. The reasons for this immense popularity, unheard of for a British poet, are complex. Partly it is a function of the intimate relationship between poetry and suffering. Modest and frail as a single poem may be, poetry is also, like grass, a perennial genus, versatile, self-seeding and nourishing. Like grass, poetry grows in the desert cave of a prison cell, in the marshes of despair, and in the wildflower meadows of the heart. And as the place where language renews itself, poetry is the garden in which our broken spirits can find deepest healing.

Poetry is thus always most popular in countries whose people suffer the worst forms of oppression.

There are also, however, culturally specific reasons for poetry's exalted status in Palestine. In the hands of Darwish and his contemporaries, Arabic poetry with its classical and oral tradition of the long poem, the lyric epic – a form both exquisite and capacious, individual and collective – became a medium *par excellence* for the expression of the magnitude of the Palestinian trauma, and the depth of the people's longing to return to their stolen land. As expressed in 'Take Care of the Stags, Father', translated by Fady Joudah in *If I Were Another*, this is a longing not death, distance or occupying army can dismember:

I am from here... I saw my guts looking upon me through the corn fuzz
I saw my memory counting the seeds of this field and the martyrs within it
I am from here. I am right here... I comb the olives in this autumn.
I am from here. And here I am. That's what my father shouted: I am from here.

Reading these long, incantatory lines, we feel a powerful tug at our own sense of attachment to place. In epic poem after poem, drawing on the ancient traditions of Arabic love poetry and other global indigenous cultures to honour his people's uprisings, dreams and defeats, Darwish conveyed the true nature of the crime of the Nakbah: a world event that goes to the heart of our shared humanity, one for which we are all responsible.

But Darwish was also legendary for his ability to reinvent both himself and Palestinian poetry. Fady Joudah notes in the poet's later period 'the shift in diction from a gnomic and highly metaphoric drive to a stroll of mixed and conversational speech', an ambulant migration that also saw Darwish scuffing the formal borders of poetry and prose. Presented here in Josh Calvo's tensile translations, new versions of late work distinguished by their taut music and startling verbs, the master's prose-poems merge lyric reflections with meta-reportage and spontaneous diary entry. Similarly, new Palestinian poetry as a whole has come to be characterised by an increasing and engaging use of colloquial speech. In part, as Maya Abu Al-Hayyat contends in her introduction to *A Bird is Not a Stone*, this change reflects a post-Oslo Accord disenchantment with old metaphors and symbols. Yet though the times are drained of beauty and, in Calvo's arresting phrase, a weary Darwish might write of an autumnal summer's day as 'a prosaic poem', figurative language is inherent in the nature of poetry: any 'poetic dictionary' contains, Borges-like, a hundred invisible definitions for every one inked on the page. Though thankfully retiring stale tropes, not least the problematic association of 'land' and 'woman', contemporary Palestinian poets are not abandoning their lyric tradition but challenging, augmenting and invigorating it. As Nathalie Handal observes, 'Palestinian letters today is a composite of vast thematic, stylistic, and linguistic traditions', and reflecting its vanguard nature as a global enterprise, the poetry collected here performs a dynamic, mixed and mutable aesthetic, a cascade of registers, lexicons, and modes of address.

Nowhere is this hybrid aesthetic more evident than in the work of Ashraf Fayadh. Based in Saudi Arabia, where his parents settled as refugees, Fayadh, a modernising art curator, was famously convicted of apostasy by the Saudi courts in November 2015: partly on the basis of poems in his first collection *Instructions Within*, he was sentenced to be beheaded. After an international outcry, this edict was eventually commuted but Fayadh is currently appealing his new punishment of eight years and eight hundred lashes. His quixotic, anguished, restless poems, lurching as they do between candid confessions and gross bodily functions, bald political truths and an implosive lyric impulse, interrogate poetry as much as power. When Fayadh uses a metaphor – 'the freedom shoe' – he labels it, brands it in a mockery of poetic aspiration. But his poems, which Waleed al-Bazoon and I have translated, also achieve a touching intimacy, their raw grief and despair tempered by a Herculean effort at respectful communication with the other. Efforts continue toward his release, and a percentage of profits from this anthology will be donated to English PEN on his behalf.

Fayadh's imprisonment is not unique. Poetry's power to unite and inspire people makes poets a potent threat to repressive regimes everywhere. Poems can be reproduced easily and cheaply, memorised, chanted in protest: in countries where freedom of expression has been whittled away, poetry can spread like wildfire – and is therefore vigorously stamped out by the state. Given that over forty percent of Palestinian males have spent time in Israeli prison, and any outspoken woman runs the same risk, it is not surprising that another poet in this book, Dareen Tatour, is currently incarcerated. As evident in a poem written for International Women's Day 2013, translated here by Andrew Leber, Tatour, of Reineh near Nazareth, is a poet of passionate nationalist and feminist concerns. In October 2015, she was arrested and indicted with incitement to violence for a poem she posted on YouTube. Although Zionist poets have never been prosecuted for incitement, and tens of thousands of recorded instances of Jewish Israeli hate speech go practically unnoticed by the Israeli justice system, Tatour has been tried and kept under house arrest until the end of the proceedings, when she faces a possible eight year jail term.[2]

The contentious poem, 'Resist, My People, Resist Them', painstakingly translated by Tariq Al Haydar from audio on the internet, calls on Palestinians to 'follow the caravan of martyrs', a phrase that may alarm some readers. Blogger and activist Yoav Haifawi – who helps Tatour communicate with the world while she is denied access to the internet – explains, however, that the line underscores the deceptive nature of translation. The prosecution's case rests on the highly emotive transliteration of the Arabic word *shahid*, the plural of which was rendered in the Hebrew translation of the poem as *shahidim*, a Hebraicization which most Jewish Israelis automatically and erroneously conflate with 'terrorists'. But *shahid* in fact has various dictionary definitions, including 'one who has fallen in battle', 'martyr', and 'victim', and should be properly 'to martyr', in Hebrew '*halal*'. Tatour's poem, the defence contended, was not a call to violence, but a commemoration of victims. A relevant interpretation of the line can only be arrived at in the context of the poem as a whole, and in fact the three individuals alluded to in the poem were all recent innocent victims of Israeli violence: sixteen year old Muhammed Abu Khdeir, kidnapped and burned alive by Israeli settlers, the infant Ali Dawabsheh, killed, as were his parents, in an settler arson attack on his home, and Hadeel Al-Hashlamoun, shot at an army checkpoint, a killing Amnesty International views as extrajudicial.

Plugged into the newsfeed and spitting out sparks, Tatour's poems make sparse but potent use of poetic imagery, invoking the classical tradition with references to caravans and fragrant agar-wood. That tradition, with its roots in pre-Islamic *Jahili* poetry, infuses the work of Marwan Makhoul, translated here by Raphael Cohen. Steeped in manna and cedar, Makhoul's 'Nocturne' is an erotic poem that creates its own candle-light. But the poet, renowned for his expressive readings, exerts virtuosic control over diverse forms and tones. 'An Arab at Ben-Gurion Airport', a Kafka-esque lyric mini-epic set in Israel's notoriously racist airport, erupts in a *tour de force* of humour, sensuality, history, anger and pride no Israeli soldier can prevent from travelling on. Though sometimes disembarking early is the only option, as Makhoul suggests in a notepad vignette of a train journey cut short by a literally rude ending.

Repression can also be felt from within a culture, and metaphor can be a weapon against such social restrictions on self-expression. In 'The Lost Button', translated by Anna Murison and Sarah Maguire, the Gazan poet Fatena Al Ghorra uses sartorial imagery to slyly explore the topic of female sexuality – taboo in not just her own society. Al Ghorra is also bold, however, offering Waleed Al-Bazoon and me the riveting experience of translating two dramatic new poems in which blood and fury spill over the boundaries between men and women, love and war, fertility and wound, body and soul. In 'I am your opponent', anguished accusations adhere to the reader, who must confront the uncomfortable possibility that the poem expresses the pain and fury of all those who, shut out of power, go unheard and untended in our globalised world. Yet the speaker's intimate recriminations stick also – and perhaps ultimately – to God.

Concerned with poetry's place in a world of mass media, and driven by the desire to confront reality directly, Maya Abu Al-Hayyat writes poems of lucid detail, grimed with endurance. Her work, sliding on oiled tracks between resignation and refusal, storytelling and aphorism, conveys both the harsh specifics of the Palestinian situation, and the speakers' responses to our globalised world: an impotent empathy in the face of internet images of suffering, and a feminine courage, rooted in a desire to be true to her protective maternal instincts. But though the poet eschews symbolism, as Abu Al-Hayyat's co-translator, I find it difficult to let the almond blossoms in her scrupulously frank poem 'Insight' remain just petals on the street. In my mind they drift across pages and years, a new phrase in Darwish's 'white almond song'.

The allusive poetry of Mustafa Abu Sneineh, translated here by Katharine Halls, also leaves the contestable question of metaphor to the reader's aesthetic judgement. Abu Sneineh, of Jerusalem and now resident in London, bears oblique witness to Palestinian suffering in poems that mingle family history with folklore and a lightly worn erudition. His 'Emperor', a dramatic monologue pinned to the classical past, holds a mirror to Cavafy, whose Roman Senators finally, famously, admit that the 'barbarian' is a 'kind of solution'. The act of barbarism presented here, though, is no rhetorical threat, but comprehensive and final. Unsettling as the term is to encounter, with its archaic dehumanisation of the enemy, in a world in which state violence still goes, not just unchecked but rewarded, the poem subtly raises the spectre of genocide, and questions the limits of survivors' psychological endurance. Yet despite its sting the poem also remains a fable: a poem that gives voice to a bee.

Palestinian poets' modes of expression are changing, then. And so is their choice of language. Uprooted as they have been, Palestinians now write in the many languages of the diaspora, the most common undoubtedly being English, the forked tongue of the Mandate coloniser. English, for transplanted Palestinian writers, thus becomes yet another double-edged blade, both a language of exclusion, in which their history is marginalised or erased, and a shining weapon with which to pierce the barricades of Anglo-American literature, history and self-perception: not simply to insert the Palestinian narrative, but to radically change the entire structure of power, opening it up into a new, porous sense of our shared humanity. Ultimately this is a project of decolonisation, redistributing power from the false, stagnant, monocultural centres of power to the active, multifarious and long-exploited periphery.

The diasporic Palestinian poets represented here negotiate a complicated linguistic relationship between mother and other tongue. One, the New York based spoken word artist and activist Farid Bitar, writes and performs back-and-forth in Arabic and

English, translating his own work. Arabic poetry has strong oral roots, and Palestinian rappers, hip hop artists and performance poets are a natural development: just as Palestinian page poets have embraced colloquial speech, their brothers and sisters on stage urgently deploy street vernacular to "tell it like is". It is, of course, largely thanks to African-American urban culture that spoken word has become a global vehicle for indigenous resistance movements; Bitar honours this symbiosis of struggles in his acknowledgement of the wrongfully imprisoned Darby Tillis, while his voice, in his recorded work with musicians, achieves a warm brotherhood of tone with Gil Scott Heron. Rap's overt political imperatives drive his work, which, in 'Only Stones Remain', also bitingly invokes the American New Wave. Bitar's melancholic musicality draws deeply too on the Arabic lyric tradition and its intrinsic relationship with memory and silence. As Fady Joudah notes in relation to the work of Ghassan Zaqtan, for a people at risk of erasure, every act of forgetting can be felt as a betrayal. Yet the past is inevitably rewritten every day. In Bitar's haunting 'Nakbah', decades of determined remembering are distilled into the flickering admission that so many versions of the story exist it is impossible to remember them all, personal and collective memories of catastrophe evaporating like the rain that remains one of the speaker's only vivid memories of his childhood in Jericho   Defining herself as an Arab-Australian, Sara Saleh's part-Egyptian heritage testifies further to the plurality that defines contemporary Palestinian identity, while the delicacy of her poems on the page veils her record as an international spoken word Slammer. A writer who communicates in English, Saleh collaborated with fellow Palestinian poet Wejdan Shamala to provide Arabic versions of impressionistic, itinerant poems that acknowledge many homes and none, speaking to the pain of dislocation and the yearning for connection, but also to youth on a global voyage of self-discovery – a thematic tension that resonates like the plangent overtones of the pear-shaped oud Saleh so poignantly celebrates.

Naomi Shihab Nye, a resident of San Antonio, is the daughter of a Swiss-German American mother and a Palestinian father, a refugee who imbued her with an indelible sense of her own history, and of the importance of kindness. A prominent voice, she is well known in the UK for a nomadic body of work that treasures the texture of everyday life and approaches the world in a profound spirit of friendship. Conversational and compassionate, Shihab Nye's poems sound the cadences of sincerity and trust, building companionship with the reader through a constant undercurrent of empathy that extends here, in 'Amir & Anna', to Israeli Jews. When violence erupts, as inevitably it must in the work of this deeply politically engaged poet, it is all the more shocking for the supple dignity of her voice, rendered here in Arabic by Raphael Cohen and Ahmed Taha.

Also based in Texas, Fady Joudah is another transatlantic literary figure whose poetry and translations have won with many prizes. A doctor and humanitarian medic, Joudah addresses the sprawling realities of global injustice and Palestinian identity with a restive, scintillating precision: his three collections vigilantly circle themes of disappearance, loss and return, and, in poems about the speakers' children, legacy. Elliptical, compelling and formally innovative, Joudah's poetry, self-translated here, performs unexpected leaps and disarming admissions. Capable of seamlessly grafting scientific terminology into meditative verse, Joudah has also replied to our technological age with the 'Textu', a 160 character poem composed on his mobile phone: mindful of phone charges in developing countries, the Textu must fit all the world's injustices, disappointments and consolations in one old Nokia screen.

Responding to the bombardment of Gaza, Deema K. Shehabi was drawn to the renga, the collaborative precursor of the haiku, co-authoring a book of the linked form, *Diaspo/Renga* with distinguished poet and translator Marilyn Hacker. In 'Gaza Renga' a harrowing sequence of memories flashes from an almost meta-physical smoke – a grief so pervasive it can never be fully described. Elsewhere Shehabi creates a subtle tissue of conflicted histories, damaged beauty and family tensions, in which a female speaker responds with a tense blend of sensuality and silence to the harsh decrees of religion and state. In these longer poems of beguiling lyricism Shehabi calls to mind, once more, Darwish, and yet another of his definitions of poetry, rendered by Joudah in a hermeneutic 'nut shell':

He said: It is the mysterious incident, poetry,
my friend, is that inexplicable longing
that makes a thing into a spectre, and
makes a spectre into a thing. Yet it might also explain
our need to share public beauty...

Certainly when I read Palestinian poetry I feel an irrepressible urge to share it. This book in your hands is the result of that need. Here in its pages are the poets of *A Blade of Grass*, Palestinians with a collective history of unfathomable loss, facing an uncertain future, speaking from their shared condition, not in one voice but, like a thirteen-stringed oud, in complex harmonics. One is no longer with us, but I hope Mahmoud Darwish would have given this book his blessing. As I was editing the book I had a dream that I was sitting alone at a large round table in a Mediterranean garden. Sensing a presence, I turned to see a man at a gate in a low stone wall: Darwish, smiling. I knew then I was waiting for the poets and translators to join me. A few weeks later, I took a break from the book down by Brighton beach. As I walked alongside the tangle of sea plants that line the old Volks railway, for the first time in my life a butterfly, a monarch, alit on me – twice. Back home, thinking Darwish would have something to say about that, I opened at random his last book of poems, *A River Dies of Thirst*, to find myself one page away from the poem 'The butterfly effect' – a mysterious power that conveys 'the lightness of the eternal in the everyday'. I believe the poems in this book, which have flown in from around the globe, have the butterfly effect. I hope they will alight on your sleeve too, delicate heralds of beauty and endurance, flitting between worlds we all, in the end, share.

Naomi Foyle, September 2017

[1] The Darwish quote from which this book's title is taken was cited by Natalie Handal in her May 2002 interview with the poet, published in *The Progressive*.
[2] Dareen Tatour's case is covered in "'With Furious Cruelty": Palestinian Poet Dareen Tatour Still Facing Prosecution in Israel' by Kim Jensen and Yoav Haifawi, *Mondoweiss*, 13 April 2017; and 'The Theatre of the Absurd: The Jewish State versus Palestinian Poet Dareen Tatour' by Yehouda Shenhav and Revital Hovel, *Haaretz*, 8 August 2017.

Works Cited

Bashir Abu-Manneh, *The Palestinian Novel: From 1948 to the Present* (CUP, 2016)

Henry Bell and Sarah Irving (eds), *A Bird is Not a Stone: An Anthology of Contemporary Palestinian Poetry* (Freight Books, 2014)

Farid Bitar, *Fatoosh* (2007), *Shutat* (2011)

Noam Chomsky and Ilan Pappé, *On Palestine* (Haymarket Books, 2015)

Mahmoud Darwish, 'Like a Mysterious Incident' in *The Butterfly's Burden* translated by Fady Joudah (Bloodaxe Books, 2007)

Mahmoud Darwish, 'Take Care of the Stags, Father' in *If I Were Another* translated by Fady Joudah (New York, 2009)

Mahmoud Darwish, 'The Butterfly Effect' in *A River Dies of Thirst* translated by Catherine Cobham (Saqi Books, 2009)

Ashraf Fayadh, *Instructions Within* translated by Mona Kareem, Jonathan Wright and Mona Zaki (Operating System, 2016)

Marilyn Hacker and Deema K. Shehabi, *Diaspo/Renga: A collaboration in alternating Renga* (Holland Park Press, 2014)

Nathalie Handal. 'The Shape of Time: New Palestinian Writing' (wordswithoutborders.org, May 2015)

Fady Joudah, *Alight* (Copper Canyon Press, 2013)

Fady Joudah, *Textu* (Copper Canyon Press, 2014)

Ghada Karmi, *Married to Another Man: Israel's Dilemma in Palestine* (Pluto Press, 2007)

Naomi Klein, 'Let Them Drown: The Violence of Othering in a Warming World' (*LRB*, June 2016)

Marwan Makhoul, *Land of the sad passion-fruit flower* (published in Arabic in Beirut, Haifa, and Cairo)

Marwan Makhoul, *Verses the poems forgot with me* (Al-Jamal Publications, 2013; 2nd edition, Dar Raya Publications) [Arabic]

Andreas Malm, 'The Walls of the Tank: On Palestinian Resistance' in *Salvage* #4 (Feb 2017)

Mazin Qumsiyeh, *Popular Resistance in Palestine: A History of Hope and Empowerment* (Pluto Press, 2011)

Deema K Shehabi, *Thirteen Departures from the Moon* (Press 53, 2011)

Naomi Shihab Nye, *Transfer* (Boa Editions, 2011)

Ghassan Zaqtan, *The Silence That Remains: Selected Poems* translated by Fady Joudah (Copper Canyon Press, 2017)

Contributors

Maya Abu Al-Hayyat is a poet, novelist, children's writer and actor, and the director of the Palestinian Writing Workshop in Birzeit. Author of three poetry collections, she won the 2006 A. M. Qattan Foundation Young Writers Award for Poetry. Born 1980 in Lebanon, she currently lives in Jerusalem with her husband and children

Mustafa Abu Sneineh is a poet and writer from Jerusalem. His first poetry collection *A Black Cloud at the End of the Line* was published in 2016. He holds a degree in Law from Birzeit University, Palestine and an MA in Postcolonial Studies from Goldsmiths College, London.

Waleed Al-Bazoon is a Senior Lecturer in English Literature at the University of Basra in Iraq. He holds a PhD in Contemporary Fiction from the University of Chichester, where he has taught in the Department of English and Creative Writing. His poetry collection *The War on Idigna* appeared in 2012.

Fatena Al Ghorra was born and educated in Gaza, where she has worked in women's projects and in journalism. The author of three poetry collections including *There is Still a Sea Between Us* (Gaza, 2000) and *A Very Troublesome Woman* (Cairo, 2003), she was a 2017 Fall Resident at the Iowa Workshop.

Tariq Al Haydar is a widely published writer whose work has appeared in *The Threepenny Review*, *Crab Orchard Review*, *The Los Angeles Review* and others. He is an assistant professor of English at King Saud University in Saudi Arabia.

Farid S. Bitar is a Palestinian-American poet, born in Jerusalem 1961. The editor of the anthology *Treasury of Arabic Love (2009)*, his own collections include *Footprints in the Mist* and two CDs *Fatoosh* and *Shutat*. *Fuzzy Lines – 67/48*, a collection of poems and paintings, is forthcoming in 2018.

Josh Calvo is a PhD student in Comparative Literature at Princeton University, where he works between Hebrew and Arabic literature. He was born into a Syrian Jewish family in New Jersey, where he encountered and first fell in love with both languages. Outside of academia, he writes short stories and novels.

Raphael Cohen is a British citizen who has lived and worked in Cairo since being denied entry to Israel in 2006. He is a translator and lexicographer with an interest in computational linguistics. His published translations include Mona Prince's *So You May See* and Mohamed Salmawy's *Butterfly Wings*.

Mahmoud Darwish (1941-2008) was born in the village of al-Birwa, in the Galilee region of Palestine, but lived variously in Beirut, Ramallah, Tunis, and Paris. One of the best loved poets in the Arab world, he published more than 30 collections, and his poetry has been translated into 35 languages. Named a Knight of the Order of Arts and Letters by France (1993), Darwish was awarded the Lannan Cultural Freedom Prize (2001), the Prince Claus Award (2004), and the Cairo Prize for Arabic Poetry (2007).

Ashraf Fayadh was born in 1980 in Saudi Arabia into a family of refugees from Gaza. An artist and poet he has curated exhibitions of Saudi art in Europe and Saudi Arabia. In 2016, partly on the basis of poems in his first collection *Instructions Within*, he was charged with apostasy and sentenced to death, later revised to an eight-year prison term and 800 lashes. His second collection, written in jail, is forthcoming in Arabic.

Naomi Foyle is an award-winning poet, novelist, verse dramatist, and essayist. Her books include *The Night Pavilion*, an Autumn 2008 Poetry Book Society Recommendation, and *The Gaia Chronicles*, a science fantasy quartet. In 2017 she co-translated *Wounds of the Cloud* by Yasser Khanger (Al Ma'mal Foundation, Jerusalem).

Katharine Halls is a freelance translator who specialises in theatre and film. She studied Hebrew and Arabic and holds an MA in Arabic-English translation and interpreting. Her co-translation, with Adam Talib, of Raja Alem's *The Dove's Necklace*, winner of the 2001 International Prize for Arabic Fiction, appeared in 2016.

Fady Joudah is the author of four poetry collections, including *The Earth in the Attic*, which was selected for the Yale Series of Younger Poets. His awards and honours include a Guggenheim Fellowship and a 2013 Griffin Poetry Prize for his translation of *Like A Straw Bird It Follows Me, and Other Poems*, by Ghassan Zaqtan.

Belal Khaled, born 1992 in Khan Younis, Gaza, is a muralist, calligrapher, graffiti artist and photojournalist. He has worked on international collaborative projects, and his art has been featured in media outlets including the *New York Times,* the *Guardian* and *Al Jazeera.*

Andrew Leber is a PhD Student at Harvard University's Graduate School of Arts and Sciences, Department of Government. His translations have appeared in *Guernica,* the *New Statesman,* and AGNI online, in addition to edited volumes of Sudanese and Iraqi fiction.

Sarah Maguire is the founder and director of the Poetry Translation Centre and the author of four highly-acclaimed collections of poetry, including *The Pomegranates of Kandahar,* a Poetry Book Society Choice that was short-listed for the TS Eliot Prize, 2007. In June 2008, Sarah received a prestigious Cholmondeley Award.

Marwan Makhoul was born 1979 in the village of Bqe'ah in the Upper Galilee to a Palestinian father and Lebanese mother. A Christian Palestinian citizen of Israel, his poetry reflects a complex identity and fierce pride as an Arab poet and man. He is a graduate in civil engineering and a practising civil engineer.

Anna Murison took an MA in Arabic from the School of Oriental and African Studies having obtained her first degree in Arabic at the University of Edinburgh. Her particular area of interest is modern Iraqi poetry.

Sara Saleh is an Arab-Australian human rights advocate, activist and writer who has spent over a decade working in the humanitarian field. Co-founder of the Dubai Poetry Slam and a past Australian Poetry Slam State Finalist, Sara has performed and published her poetry internationally. Her first poetry collection is *Wasting the Milk in the Summer*.

Wejdan Shamala is a Palestinian New Zealander youth support worker for refugee communities in Australia. She has an academic background in International Relations, as well as Education & Development Studies.

Deema K. Shehabi is a widely published poet, writer and editor. She grew up in the Arab world and attended college in the US, where she received an MS in journalism. Her debut collection *Thirteen Departures from the Moon* was followed by *Diaspo/Renga*, a collaboration with Marilyn Hacker.

Naomi Shihab Nye, a Palestinian-American resident of Texas, was born in St. Louis and lived in Jerusalem in her youth. She has written or edited more than 30 books of poetry and prose for young readers and adults, including *Habibi, Sitti's Secrets, 19 Varieties of Gazelle*, and *The Turtle of Oman*.

Ahmed Taha is a leading poet of the 1970's generation in Egypt. He founded the poetry movement Aswat, which in 1988 produced *Black Writing* magazine; and in 1994 he published the magazine *Locusts*, launching the 1990's generation of Egyptian poets. His poetic works include: *Table 48, Empire of Walls,* and *Bustan Passageway.*

Dareen Tatour is a poet and photographer from Reineh in the Galilee. Her rebellious poems challenge the occupation, social injustice and the fate of women. On October 2015 she was arrested and indicted for incitement, mostly about a poem. She is still under house arrest pending the end of the trial. Her prosecution aroused worldwide condemnation.

Acknowledgements

I am grateful to Andy Croft of Smokestack Books for the invitation to edit this anthology, and to all the contributors for the opportunity to work with them, an experience from which many valued friendships have emerged. I thank especially Waleed Al-Bazoon, Josh Calvo and Raphael Cohen for their commitment to the Arabic translations, and Josh also for his keen eye on the proofs; Mustafa Abu Sneineh for his editorial work on those translations, and his perspicacious comments on the Introduction; Fatena Al Ghorra and Maya Abu Al-Hayyat for the illuminating Skype calls; and Fady Joudah for his critical insights. I thank also Rewa' Attieh for translating the Call for Submissions; Merna Azzeh for her invaluable help with the Arabic typesetting; Zamzam Bayian for her help with transcription; Haim Bresheeth, Yosefa Loshitsky and Marilyn Hacker for recommending poets to me; Yoav Haifawi for ensuring I correctly reported Dareen Tatour's case; Pete Langman for his copyediting skills; M. Lynx Qualey, Sarah Irving and Mazin Qumsiyeh for their support of the crowdfunding campaign, and Ben Noys at the University of Chichester for alerting me to the Andreas Malm article quoted in the Introduction.

I am grateful to Mona Kareem for her permission to translate and publish new work by Ashraf Fayadh, from his forthcoming collection *Sick Histories*. All previously published work by living poets has been republished with permission of the poets. 'The Lost Button' by Fatena Al Ghorra was first published on the website of the Poetry Translation Centre (UK). 'Resist, My People, Resist Them', 'A Poet Behind Bars', 'I... Who Am I?' were all previously published as blogposts from *Arabic Literature (in English)*. 'Green Flies', 'Like a Prosaic Poem', 'Beyond my identity' and 'Nero' were first published in *Diaries* (*Yawmiyyat*) by Mahmoud Darwish (*al-Karmel*, Summer 2006). Of Fady Joudah's poems, 'Mimesis' and 'Twice a River' were first collected in *Alight* (Copper Canyon Press, 2013); while 'Darwish', 'Revenge', 'Believe', 'Thank You Dark World', 'I Only Want From Love' and 'Authenticity Bargain' first appeared in *Textu* (Copper Canyon Press, 2014). Of Marwan Makhoul's poems, 'On the Tel Aviv Train' was previously published in *Land of the sad passion-fruit flower* (2011, Beirut, Haifa and Cairo), while 'An Arab in Ben-Gurion Airport' and 'Nocturne' are taken from his collection *Verses the poems forgot with me* (Al-Jamal Publications, Baghdad/Beirut; and Dar Raya Publications, Haifa, 2013). Of Naomi Shihab Nye's poems, 'Talking Forever' was first published on the website of Jewish Voice for Peace (USA); 'Everything in Our World Did Not Seem to Fit', 'Thirst' and 'Amir & Anna' were first collected in *Transfer* (BOA Editions, 2011). All efforts were made to acquire relevant institutional permissions; in the event of any omissions, please contact Smokestack Books to rectify the acknowledgements for the next edition.

A University of Chichester Research Development Award enabled a fee to be paid to all the contributors. Thanks to the generosity of the following contributors to the book's crowd-funding campaign, Smokestack Books was able to increase that fee and make significant donations to the legal funds of Ashraf Fayadh and Dareen Tatour. *Shukran jazilan*, everyone!

Olive Branch Donors
Deb Barnard, Owen Cooper, Helen Dixon, Ella Elbaz-Nir, Max Farrar, Sara Gowen, Julian Molina Guillen, Rahila Gupta, Rob Hamberger & Keith Rainger, Dan Hass, Sarah Irving, Wendy Klein, Jacob Melish, Geraldine Mitchell, Seni Seneviratne and Diana Shelley.

Kanafeh Donors
Seamus Cashman, Dr Araf N. Dajani, Marilyn Hacker, Sarah Hymas, Jeff Seneviratne, Lee Whitaker and Eliza Wyatt.

Qabbeh Donors
Rowyda Amin, Anthony Litwinko and Hilary Smith.

Sahja Donor
Ibrahim Al-Salti

Plus 19 others who wished to remain anonymous.

Marwan Makhoul

An Arab at Ben-Gurion Airport

I am Arab!
I yell at the entrance to the airport.
To shorten the woman soldier's path
I go up to her and say: Interrogate me! But
quick, if you don't mind. I don't want to miss
departure time.

She says: Where are you from?

From the Ghassassanian kings of Golan comes my chivalry, I reply.
Neighbour of a harlot from Jericho
who gave Judah the wink on his way to the West Bank
the day he occupied the land that the front page of history
occupied after him.
My answers indurate as Hebron granite:
I was born in the time of the Moabites who came before you
to this submissive land of ages.
From Canaan my father
and my mother from South Lebanon, once a Phoenician.
Her mother, my mother's, died two months ago:
without a final farewell to her mother's body, my mother,
   two months ago,
I wept in her arms so that sympathy in Buqaya might console her
on the foothills of tragedy and fate:
Lebanon, impossible sister, and me,
my mother's lone mother
in the north!

She asks me: Who packed your bag for you?

I say: Osama bin Laden! But
Easy now – it's the harmless humour of the hurt,
a joke realists like me use professionally here
in the fight.

I've struggled sixty years talking words of peace;
I don't attack settlements
and I don't have tanks like you do,
ridden by soldiers to chew up Gaza.
Firing bombs from an Apache isn't on my CV,
not out of a shortcoming in me,
but because I see on the horizon the echo of frustration
at a misplaced non-violent revolution
and good behaviour.

Did anyone give you something on the way here? she asks.

An exile from Nayrab refugee camp
gave me memories
and the key to a house from the fabled past.
The rust on the key made me edgy, but I'm
like stainless steel, I compose self with self should I grow nostalgic,
for the groans of refugees
spread wings of longing across borders.
No guard can stop it, nor thousands
and not you for sure.

She says: Do you have any sharp implements in your possession?

I answer: My passion
my skin, my olive complexion
my being born here in innocence, but for fate.
Pess-optimistic I was in the seventies
but I'm optimistic about the roars of disobedience
right now being raised to you in Gilboa gaol.
I'm straight out of the tragic
novels of history, the end of the story
a funeral for the past and a wedding

in the not far-off hall of hope.
A date from the Jordan Valley raised me
and taught me to speak.
I have a child whose due date I postpone, so he'll arrive
to a morning not made of straw like today, Ukrainian girl.
I have the muezzin's chant to move me, even though I'm an atheist.
I shout to mute the mournful wailing of the flutes,
to turn pistols into the undying refrain of violins.

The soldier leads me off to search my things
ordering me to open my bag.
I do what she wants!
And from the depths of the bag bubble up my heart and my song,
the meaning of it all slips out eloquently and crudely, within it all
    that is me.

She asks me: And what's this?

I say: The sura of the Night Journey ascending the ladder of my
    veins,
the Tafsir of Jalalayn, the poetry of Abu Tayyeb al-Mutannabi
and my sister Maram,as a photograph and real at the same time,
a silk shawl to enwrap and protect me from the chilling exile of
    relatives,
tobacco from a kiosk in Arraba that made my head spin until
    doubts got stoned.
Inside me a fierce loyalty, the wild thyme of my country,
the flame of pomegranate blossoms, Galilean and sparkling.
Inside me agate, camphor-wood, incense and my vitality,
the pearl that is Haifa: scintillating, everlasting, illuminating,
transforming, resting in the pocket of our return for one reason
only: we worshipped our good intentions and bound
the Nakba to a mistake in the past and in me!

The soldier hands me over to a policeman
who pats me down and shouts in surprise:
What's this!?

The manhood of my nation, I say
and my progeny, the fold of my family and two dove's eggs
to hatch, male and female, from me and for me.
He searches me
for anything that could pose a threat
but this stranger is blind
forgetting the more grievous and important devices within:
my spirit, my defiance, the swoop of the eagle in my breath and my
  body
my birthmark and my valour. That is me
whole and complete in a way this fool
will never see.

Now, after two hours of psychological grappling
I lick my wounds for a sufficient five minutes
then embark on the plane that has taken off. Not to leave
and not to return
but to see the woman soldier below me,
the policeman in the national anthem of my shoes below me,
and below me a big lie of tin-can history
like Ben-Gurion become as always, as always, as always
below me.

Translated by Raphael Cohen

Nocturne

Evening with you is sweetened night,
as if like the evergreen laurel
you exuded droplets of dew
that at dawn I wake and shake off
before morning opens an eye or yawns and stretches.

Evening with you is manna and quail,
a red-hot coal beneath the kindling of feelings
that bursts into you the flame.
My body on top of you softens just before melting.
Now will you let me write my own elegy,
and shower into sparks?

Evening with you is a *fatwa*
and a tender Lord who treasures me.
I become the believer who makes pilgrimage
from you unto you, and worships.

Evening with you is sanctuary
and a river of musk pouring over me
as if I were rushes bending down at the river
to drink and be sated.

Come let us try to cross the gulf
between poles of separation on horses of instinct,
or do we dare the distance, far-cedar of Paradise,
where our fortune must turn
and shine for us.

Come near me!
Because parting glowers evil over us.
Come near me! Then parting will swoon to be forgotten.
Come near me, and all is forgotten.

Evening with you is a wolf yet more cunning,
a wolf that pounced on the gazelle of my soul,
caught staring at her beauty in the mirror
of a spring's waters making herself beautiful,
seemingly clearer and sweeter.

Evening with you is a wolf yet dumber
for if in attack he had held back
he would have kissed the prey on the cheek
then tasted what would become on reflection
more delicious than gazelle and more desirable.

Translated by Raphael Cohen

On the Tel Aviv Train

On the train to Tel Aviv
I saw her...
a Russian signifying the essence of mint.
She had all of Moscow in her hand
and a child
who seemed Middle Eastern.

In the same carriage, an Ethiopian
stared at the faces of the passengers
stared until he grew bored of them
then looked out of the window
at a ruined Arab village that held no interest.

A worker and recent immigrant sat
lively, since he would shortly get off
the train for his shift at a factory
that had just laid him off.

To my right sat a Jew
from Morocco who told me his woes
until he twigged to my accent.
He kept on talking, but
with the person to his right.

I got off at the next station
because the poem stopped.

Translated by Raphael Cohen

Dareen Tatour

Resist, My People, Resist Them

Resist, my people, resist them.
In Jerusalem, I dressed my wounds and breathed my sorrows
And carried the soul in my palm
For an Arab Palestine.
I will not succumb to the 'peaceful solution,'
Never lower my flags
Until I evict them from my land.
I cast them aside for a coming time.
Resist, my people, resist them.
Resist the settler's robbery
And follow the caravan of martyrs.
Shred the disgraceful constitution
Which imposed degradation and humiliation
And deterred us from restoring justice.
They burned blameless children;
As for Hadil, they sniped her in public,
Killed her in broad daylight.
Resist, my people, resist them.
Resist the colonialist's onslaught.
Pay no mind to his agents among us
Who chain us with the peaceful illusion.
Do not fear doubtful tongues;
The truth in your heart is stronger,
As long as you resist in a land
That has lived through raids and victory.
So Ali called from his grave:
Resist, my rebellious people –
Write me as prose on the agarwood;
My remains have you as a response.
Resist, my people, resist them.
Resist, my people, resist them.

Translated by Tariq Al Haydar

A Poet Behind Bars

Jelemeh Prison, 2 November 2015 (the day I was indicted)

In prison, I met people
too numerous to count:
Killer and criminal,
thief and liar,
the honest and those who disbelieve,
the lost and confused,
the wretched and the hungry.
Then, the sick of my homeland,
born out of pain,
refused to comply with injustice
until they became children whose innocence was violated.
The world's compulsion left them stunned.
They grew older.
No, their sadness grew,
strengthening in repression,
like roses in salted soil.
They embraced love without fear,
and were condemned, not
for their deeds, but for declaring,
'We love the land endlessly,'
so their love freed them.
See, prison is for lovers.
I interrogated my soul
during moments of doubt and distraction:
'What of your crime?'
Its meaning escapes me now.
I said the thing and
revealed my thoughts;
I wrote about the current injustice,
wishes in ink,
a poem I wrote...
The charge has worn my body,
from my toes to the top of my head,

for I am a poet in prison,
a poet in the land of art.
I am accused of words,
my pen the instrument.
Ink – blood of the heart – bears witness
and reads the charges.
Listen, my destiny, my life,
to what the judge said:
A poem stands accused,
my poem morphs into a crime.
In the land of freedom,
the artist's fate is prison.

Translated by Tariq Al Haydar

I... Who am I?

The wind asks... who am I?
You are Me,
Voice of mine.
I am the woman of the Departed One,
He who was wronged on that foggy night,
Or write, instead, the woman of the Transformed One.
I walk ahead without a step to either side,
I desire the life that exists in Nowhere,
I go on, as my ghost has no desire to remain.
My freedom...
Lies in the sound of women.

The sea asks... who am I?
I am the pearl buried in the heart of the deep,
The patience embedded in the sands of time.
I am Me...
A storm of angry waves at sunset,
Its breathing strangled in the grip of each gust.
But as I draw near the question pulls away,
And I keep on asking: 'Who am I?'

A nation asks... who am I?
I am Here.
Brought forth from a womb of misery,
A child encircled by pain,
A teardrop shackled by anger.
I am the very love of the nation.
I have lived in this land,
Growing up in the byways of Nazareth,
Which became a song of peace for the birth of desires.
And I remained here, steadfast,
Building for Nazareth an eternal dream.

The palm tree asks... who am I?
I am just like him.
Against the sun, standing tall.
I rise up, my shadow standing there,
On the ground before me. I will not die,
Unless amputated, uprooted from my crying out
The sound of silence.

The soul asks... who am I?
I am the confession of the conscience.
A person who reveals the question:
Am I living among reality?
Or am I a phantasm of imagination?
I am confused in a world that has sold its beliefs,
One now covered over in devastation.
Life itself, come, drink and slake your thirst –
For the clouds will come to revitalize us.

Translated by Andrew Leber

Maya Abu Al-Hayyat

I'm a destitute woman

Who lives on a checkpoint
Trivial things make me happy
As when my day passes without seeing a single bored soldier
I write my new novel there
About the butcher who wanted to become a violinist
Mad and evil
But his hand failed him
For a sharp, shiny knife
You know how bleak it is
To be alone and living on a checkpoint
Cheering for simple things
As if to transcend a chattering poet
And exhausted labourers carrying bags
Of bananas, guava and tnuva milk
I'm a solitary woman
Who's lived in a grave for years
So far I haven't seen any demons or angels
But I definitely see a lot of bored soldiers

Translated by Maya Abu Al-Hayyat and Naomi Foyle

Painful pictures

I will tell you about the painful pictures
In the cold

1
Twenty men
In old leather coats
Gamblers in cheap sportswear
Faces exude beards, pain and cold
Mouths wrapped in hands and plates and scarves
Snow falls on everything
The sentence below reads
'Syrians waiting in the cold and rain to buy bread'
With an invitation to see more photos
I do not enter
I'm no saint
I'm just a bored person
Who browses painful images
To cry a little and thank God
For the blessing of a warm house
Then put more rags on the window
To stop the wind whistling

2
'For more painful images please click here'

Translated by Maya Abu Al-Hayyat and Naomi Foyle

Insight

I am waiting for a brave martyr's daughter
To stand up and scream
Take your homeland
And give me back my dad

The almond blossom knows its life is short
But the bud cracks and yawns
And only when it falls on the streets of the school
Does happiness bloom

All the minutes of silence
Cannot return one voice to life

I've lived a life filled with heroes
And complete bastards
Now I can no longer distinguish between them

I have seen children
Who gave their parents to the homeland
But I have never seen a homeland
That gave an orphan a father

I want everyone to live and no one to fall
Not even my demons
Not even your demons
Maybe if not one of us falls
We will all rise
Above this hell

Translated by Maya Abu Al-Hayyat and Naomi Foyle

Whistling

Do you see the hole in my neck?
I no longer remember whether it was from a bullet or a word
But I am sure that two lips have passed through it
And left their whistle
Behind
That is why you hear this rattle
Whenever I turn to look back on the past
Or forward to the future

Translated by Maya Abu Al-Hayyat and Naomi Foyle

I cannot believe the common grief

Nor love in public
I cannot believe the endless talking about justice
Nor the talking about conviction
If you are not a bit wicked
I will know that you are very wicked
There are things
That can't be true

Translated by Maya Abu Al-Hayyat and Naomi Foyle

Fatena Al Ghorra

The Lost Button

This morning, the shop windows look drab.
People hurry straight past the gaudy dresses.
Mirrors lined-up on the pavement wait for reflections.
The streets still deserted,
the sticky palms of passers-by are lined with sleep.
Then a solitary shirt
gapes wide open on the path -
what cast you in front of these mirrors?
Morning lifts from the heavy eyes of those wandering
    aimlessly.
Only the shirt knows their face.
Only the shirt –
yet their only pleasure is bargaining.
The shirt shivers in anticipation,
longing for someone who cares nothing for prices,
who knows nothing of sucking the desire from a button,
a button half-hidden, stitched to a label, lost in the folds
    of cloth:
the button touches itself and lets out a sigh of relief.
It was when her hand moved across the window
that she found this lost button.
Alert, lost in thought, she forgets the strangers passing
    her by.
She flushes with tenderness, with the secret aftermath
    of desire,
dazzling the window.

Translated by Anna Murison and Sarah Maguire

I am your opponent

Try to open your mouth in my direction
To let all the black holes out from my inside
You are opening a door for me and cruelly closing it
Loosening your castles and freeing your masts for prayers
Standing confused before my orphan prayer

I am your opponent
The demanding, the pleading, the blaming and refusing,
The disappointed, the sinner, the exhausted one and the troublemaker
You have your excuses
That I am naïve and that my vision too narrow
I know this answer very well and I am ready to defend myself from it
I want my wings
But you never stop interfering, never stop
Sowing my path with traps
Well, I have no problem with that
Except that your eternal promises to me
– that this chaos will stop one day –
never come true.

I am your opponent
Who is fragmented from inside
Like a piece of crystal pasted after being broken

I am the loud crying one, and the sprawling laughter
I come to you protected by my own compelling excuses
My own irrefutable accusations
Your opponent is lying down now
In a dark corner staring at the road
My strong and intermittent gasps almost uprooting this blooded heart
I am waiting for the moment when there are no passersby
To go out and howl

Howling in your face and on you and on life
That bitch
I will never stop howling
I will never stop kicking or cursing
Untill you come to me and tell me
Why you kneaded my heart in this leaky bowl
And left it eaten with holes
Like a smugglers' crossing for out-of-date goods
I will not stop howling
And you answer that the dough was softer than you expected
And the ingredients incomplete
So you shaped it with clay and soft winter grass
In order that, whenever it is nearly dry
It will seep its water

Translated by Waleed Al-Bazoon and Naomi Foyle

Blood

Red as it should be
Flowing like that
Drilling in my soul a place for screaming
Flowing as if an explosion
Leaving carnage behind
It keeps flowing without boredom or forgiveness
When its scream convulses my body
It takes part of my soul
Exactly red
It does not compromise with colour or with pain
Fissuring its way as if it had dug it
It does not bargain
Doesn't give a shit
For compassion or temporary pain
Blood
Dark red
Splitting my soul into two halves
Messing up my papers
And my dealings with others
Sufficing with a thunderous fingerprint
I like sometimes to put my finger
In that small crack
To stop the flowing
Or maybe to know from where and how it comes!
Its dark red colour
Its pain that my soul cannot endure and is not saved from
Except by an anesthetic
Placing my fingers simply and quietly
I let the river run
Warm, flowing, dark
Sated with lost lust
It smells like the laundry of a countryside woman
With a scent of blue flower and chlorine that penetrates the nose
Sneaking into the whole body
Giving it nectar, unsurpassable

It comes just like that
A fragrance clinging to the soul and sealing it
You can see it clear on the landmarks of the body
Pleasant, different, calling
Like a hungry she-wolf waiting for its prey
A smell that does not carry many names
Penetrating the soul
Carrying the body to the desire
That eats everything, the green and the dry,
And the foetus in its first cradle
The blood comes just like that
With a colour that mystifies the painters in its structure
With shapes on the face and in the flesh
That cannot be grasped except by an expert...
Blood that every night awaits the cry of the wolf to declare its
    existence
Its cadence is difference
Sometimes it comes generous, penetrating, flushed with power
Leaving no space for breathing or looking
Sometimes dark brown sneaking in difficulty, stickiness, thickness
And sometimes it feels pity for that fragile body and it comes just like
    that
With a slight pain in the soul
Almost finding no place
Forcing up its flag in a shameless
coming to life

Translated by Waleed Al-Bazoon and Naomi Foyle

Ashraf Fayadh

Stink

Writing, quite often, is like digestion.
Sometimes we are constipated.
Other times, we suffer from diarrhoea.
But the latter may produce bad texts!
It is a comfortable feeling to discharge what is inside your stomach,
or at least your large intestine.
It has nothing to do with arrogance or non-arrogance.
I mean stink.
Now I will not be able to speak about love.
There is no relation between love and stink.
Is our unawareness of smell considered a disability?
I cannot respect people too much.
The body of the woman is beautiful despite others' attempt to hide it
and limit who can enjoy it.
Enjoyment is a taboo
we hide.
Intolerance is an honour
we pretend.
Many times, killing is a source of pride!
Insofar as we may be awarded medals, wealth and titles,
it can be that we rule the world because we killed a lot of people.
All are sure they are right.
Why do I, after all that, separate love from stink?
Why do I not miss you despite my presence at the heart of a forest of
    stink?
May be it is a desire to smell another smell.
So much so that I pay money for it.
War suits stink.
They are connected.
My name increases in strangeness.
Do you understand what I mean?

Sometimes I write in a pleasant handwriting,
sometimes I write in a terrible handwriting.
Sometimes I love you.
And other times I love you!
I mean, when I am angry with you.
So angry that nothing else exists to be angry about.
I am not angry with you as a person.
But I am angry with you because of your behaviours.
You know I do not want you to change anything about you.
Because I loved you just like that...
I am ready to be angry to the utmost.
I will keep on loving you.
You will keep on loving my anger with your behaviours.
The circle does not end... like the universe...
Like the rotation of planets around their moody suns...
Like your smile last time!

Translated by Waleed Al-Bazoon and Naomi Foyle

Cracked Skin

My country passed through here
Wearing the freedom shoe.
It went far away, leaving its shoe behind.
It was running in a confused rhythm, like the beat of my heart.
My heart, which was running in another direction, with no
    convincing reason!
The freedom shoe was torn, old and fake,
Like human values in all their dimensions.
Everything left me behind and went away including you.
The shoe is a confusing invention.
It proves our ineligibility to live on this planet.
It proves we belong to another place, where we do not need to
    walk for long,
Maybe its floor is paved with cheap slippery ceramics.
The problem is not with slipperiness, but with water.
The problem of heat, broken glass, thorns, dry branches, sharp
    rocks.
The shoe is not an ideal solution...
But it satisfies certain of our purposes,
Exactly like the mind,
Like emotion.
My emotion is dead since you left me last time.
I cannot reach you since my imprisonment
inside a cement box engraved with cold metal rods.
Since everyone forgot me, starting with my freedom,
ending with my shoes which suffer from an identity crisis.

Translated by Waleed Al-Bazoon and Naomi Foyle

Offline

Have we finished?
I am no longer able to send such a message.
Did you notice the difference?
Do you think that this is a natural result?
In one regard, it is not natural:
It should have happened a long time ago, a long long time ago.
You will arm yourself with silence as you used to do,
Busying yourself with reading Kafka, or maybe Sartre!
Damn both Kafka and Sartre, and Umru al-Qais.
Though the questions of the latter were not discussed in a
    serious way,
Maybe because he was addicted to alcohol,
Or because his long night has not yet finished.
For me too, the morning does not especially deserve to be
    gambled on.
Yes, I will miss your bad mood,
I will miss you completely.
What is important is that my mind obliges me to be impartial in
    my feelings towards you and
To transcend them to order to keep my ragged balance.
I do not care anymore for balance, I long to see you looking far
    away even if everything is near you.
This is what my mind does.
To this degree, it is like you.

PS:
I will no longer use my heart to express love because my heart is
    very tired, so tired that it is now dedicated simply to pumping
    blood, this being the only way for it to rid itself of the power of
    the brain.
Both the heart and the brain are superpowers.
Neither can rid itself of the other because neither can survive
    without the other.
Which one would you choose to be?
Sorry, this is just a rhetorical question I wanted to ask you directly...
    before but not now.

Translated by Waleed Al-Bazoon and Naomi Foyle

Stroke

I live in hard times
Sleep behaves like a teenage girl in love for the first time
I will talk neither about the state of my heart, nor about the
    mental disorders that bubble up in me,
    beyond boiling point
I am a part of the universe that the universe got angry with
I am a part of the earth which embarrassed the earth
I am a hopeless human that other humans were unable to treat with
    impartiality
Impartiality is an illusion
Like all the virtues that people talk about in a shameless theoretical
    manner
Justice is an inexact word, exactly like human
Love moves like a hopeless fly trapped inside a glass cube
Freedom is a very relative thing
We live, in the end, in a spherical prison
Its bars are made of ozone
When we are set free from it, we face our doom, our fate, our death
I cannot laugh
I cannot even smile
I cannot, at the same time, cry
I cannot behave as a human and this does not grieve me at all
Much as it pains me
To have a body sparsely covered by hair
To walk on two feet
To be totally dependent on your mind
To be led to the brink by your own desire
To have your freedom caged
To have others decide to kill you
To miss the nearest humans to you
To miss the opportunity to say goodbye
What is the benefit of saying goodbye except to leave a sad
    impression?
What is the benefit of meeting?
What is the benefit of love?

What is the benefit of being alive in this way?
While others die of grief for you?
The last time I saw my dad was behind a thick glass
And then he went away, never to return
Let's say because of me
Let's say he couldn't tolerate the idea that I would die before him
My dad died and left death encircling me
Without me feeling afraid enough of it.
Why does death frighten us to death?
My dad departed after he had lived a long time on this planet
I did not say goodbye to him in a proper way
I did not feel sad for him properly
I was not able to cry
As is my habit which increases in ugliness with the passage of time
Policemen encircle me
In their drab uniforms
Laws, legislations and codes encircle me
Sovereignty encircles me
Living creatures cannot shed their highly concentrated instinctive
    desires
My loneliness encircles me
My loneliness chokes me
Melancholy and stress and depression disappear and regret at
    belonging to the human race kills me
I was unable to say goodbye to all my loved ones and they departed
    though temporarily
I was unable to leave a kind impression in my last meeting
Then I surrendered to the guns of longing aimed right at me
I refused to raise my hand and was not able to move
Then sadness chained me, but it failed to make me cry
Awareness eats me from the inside
Killing every chance at survival
Awareness kills me slowly
It is far too late to heal

Translated by Waleed Al-Bazoon and Naomi Foyle

Mustafa Abu Sneineh

Emperor

It isn't true, Emperor,
'That what is not good for the swarm,
is not good for the bee.'
Permit me, a bee, to set right your meditations:
I no longer have a swarm to fly with
Nor wildflowers who understand my tongue.

The hive has crumbled under the boots of the barbarians.
Traitors betrayed it
and I'd have recited prayers for its courageous soul, if I knew any.

The time of bees is over, Emperor.
Let me fly on fractured wings to another abyss
I leave behind no honey, no wax,
and the flowers I alight on jabber in the barbarians' language.

Leave me out of your meditations, for I am no good to anyone,
and it's all the same whether the swarm returns or not,
Emperor,
it's all the same.

Translated by Katharine Halls

The quotation is from the *Meditations* of Marcus Aurelius (121-180).

Straw

I'm the straw the drowning clutch at –
I confess, I'm guilty, I drowned your children.
For years I was ready to come to their aid
But no-one
ever
fell in.
I fought the fierce current, I refused hands extended, I put down roots
in what you called the swamp.
They thought me a tree-trunk,
a dry branch entreating your waning fires
And when they swam over to fish me out
I watched their foolish progress
with a crocodile's eyes.

Translated by Katharine Halls

Cell no. 8

Only my father knows
What news he heard on that little transistor.
He and a handful of comrades.
I wasn't there, in Ramle prison, to witness it.
No-one was
but my father and a few comrades.
I can only imagine the news he must have heard:
The withdrawal from Beirut
Sadat's speech in the Knesset
'We will respond appropriately'
The Tammuz reactor airstrike
This and that being a 'red line.'
I can only picture them in cell no. 8
trying to kill time with a yellow transistor,
only picture days trickling down the back of the years
as my father scores the casing
with his prisoner number.

Only my father knows the insults heaped on that yellow
transistor.
He alone knows the night and the moon, the day and the sun,
the number of stars and the shape of the clouds
in Ramle prison.
Because I wasn't there to witness.
No-one was
but my father and a few comrades.
I can only picture them in cell no. 8
rousing the morning,
pouring the sky some water from the prison tap,
can only picture the rock of victory they carried on their backs
year after year
as they listened to the news of defeat.

Translated by Katharine Halls

Nablus Street

It was a wordless confession.
I recall the sun sliding into the darkness of the settlement,
Soldiers with guns beating the sunset
until it passed out.

A lovestruck boy stealing poems from Nizar Qabbani
and love letters from *The Snow Comes Through the Window*.
I'm still a lovestruck boy –
Even though the sun has long since gone under,
Even though my first confession of love
Was made in the crosshairs of the occupation's guns.

Translated by Katharine Halls

The Snow Comes Through the Window is a novel by Syrian writer Hanna Mina.

Ant

My story is there when the story of war is told –
Since no-one pays attention to a plucky ant except
when a defeated Conqueror notices her.

I stumble, stumble, and get up again, whenever a soldier
recounts my story.
They say the language of war comes from the arsenal,
But I only know the language of the wheat
I've been carrying for years, only to stumble again.

The conqueror can stare all he likes.
One day someone will come and tell the story I recognise:
A brave ant contemplating a defeated conqueror.

Translated by Katharine Halls

Farid Bitar

O! Jericho

Driving downhill into the valley
Mountains so old Bedouins still dwell in it
Prophets walked through it
Abraham   Moses   Mohammad

Lowest point on earth
Where else can you go but up?
Childhood city of mine

Reached the famous Sea Level stone
Had to stop and kiss it
Eerie feeling
Ears popped from pressure
Wife couldn't hear
No more

Got to the outskirts of the city
Israeli border patrol
The questions started
I have been refused entry
For the past twenty-two years to be exact
Not this time   God is good
No Man's Land
Palestinian land
Salaam Allahu Aliekum (may peace be upon you)
Wa'aliekum As-salaam (and peace upon you)
Welcome home son
Guards yelled smiling
I also was smiling

Passed by the 'Head Hospital'
You see I ran away from home
At age four to look for
My father who's never home
Mother said 'Your father King of the Apple Market
Is at work'
I said in my head 'I know where that market is'
Got hit with a chicken truck
Right in front of the hospital
They scooped me up with my
Head cracked wide open

Looked for the house
I grew up in   still there
Said hello to the balcony
The one I slept in
In the very hot summer nights
Same balcony that I saw dead people from
When the enemy raped my sleepy town

Sipped mint tea
Jericho has the best mint tea on earth
Tasted the sweetest oranges on earth
Felt I'm back to my happy childhood
Felt I'm in *deja vu* land
When I smelled the rain
Evaporating in the hot summer days
Poof   gone in seconds
Where I walked through the streets
When I was my older brother's tail
Going to school   Terra Sancta

Jericho O! Jericho
Home of the Mount of Temptation
The Umayyad Winter Palaces
Home of the best lemon trees
Where I smelled the jasmine perfuming the streets
Also home of the Refugee Camps
Poverty and misery nowadays

Drove through the valley
Along the River Jordan
Where Jesus washed his feet
Drove to Tiberia Lake
Drove to Nazareth
Home of the famous prophet

Jericho O! Jericho
Home of the Dead Sea
Where nothing lives now
Even fish left town.

Nakbah

15 May 1948–6 June 1967

I have told this story

So many versions
That sometimes I forget
How it all started
An eternity away
Mother narrated the middle
I read the start

Father refrained from talking
I keep dwelling on the past
While I should build the future
The problem is
Every time I build the nest
Zion keeps destroying it

It all started a simple way
An innocent child
Growing in a sleepy town - Jericho
I still remember the mint tea
I still smell the rain evaporating.

Only Stones Remain

27 August 2014. During the 52 day invasion of Gaza
2,185 civilians were killed by Israel.

again and again
falling down on my head
and the dead are too many
to blame
only stones remain
Umm Ahmad wailing
holding a stone in one hand
hitting her face with the other
screaming,
where is my beautiful house
where is my beautiful life
where is my son I am looking for
I have his favourite toy
I found his arms
I found his legs
I can't find his head
where is my beautiful child
where is my beautiful wife
where is my beautiful house
I am not talking about
talking heads
only stones remain
again and again
falling down on my head
I will rebuild Shuja'aiya
I will rebuild every stone
I will rebuild Beit Hanoun
that al-shaytan Zion destroyed
and the dead are too
many to blame.

Pain that never heals

12 December 2012

Spoke to the birds about it
They told me 'do what we always do
Fly to another place
Then come back with a fresh start
To the same place that you started'

The olive tree was listening
Told me 'sonny don't listen to the birds
Look at me; I am in the same place for ages
I get uprooted, so the IDF soldiers can get a better view
I always resurface
I survived Empires
They are gone, I am still here'

Was listening to Darby Tillis
Spilling his guts
About his pain that never heals – 20 years now
Spent 8 years on death row in Chicago jails
For a crime that he never committed
The police made up the charges
Now exonerated
He still cries about his pain

My pain keeps getting re-opened
Every time the Israelis invade Gaza
The flotillas that never make it
My people living on a dollar a day
My pain never goes away

Naomi Shihab Nye

Everything in Our World Did Not Seem to Fit

Once they started invading us.
Taking our houses and trees, drawing lines,
pushing us into tiny places.
It wasn't a bargain or deal or even a real war.
To this day they pretend it was.
But it was something else.
We were sorry what happened to them but
we had nothing to do with it.
You don't think what a little plot of land means
till someone takes it and you can't go back.
Your feet still want to walk there.
Now you are drifting worse
than homeless dust, very lost feeling.
I cried even to think of our hallway,
cool stone passage inside the door.
Nothing would fit for years.
They came with guns, uniforms, declarations.
Life magazine said,
'It was surprising to find some Arabs still in their houses.'
Surprising? Where else would we be?
Up on the hillsides?
Conversing with mint and sheep, digging in dirt?
Why was someone else's need for a home
greater that our own need for our own homes
we were already living in? No one has ever been able
to explain this sufficiently. But they find
a lot of other things to talk about.

Thirsty

'Israelis Kill Palestinian Boy at Protest…'

Every day the stories
say 'militant' – probably
a broken-hearted boy
doing something desperate,
and I miss you. You knew.
Ahmed Moussa left too soon.
Protesting the wall
cutting off his village's olive trees
from the people who tend them,
hauling buckets of water,
the people who gather,
who sing the song of olive, all their days.
Don't go down there, begged his family.
Ten-year-old defending trees.
Who else had the patience?
Bullet in the forehead for Ahmed Moussa.
'Mourners gathered around the boy's father,
who leaned against a wall.'
Morgue wall this time.
Hold them up, Dad.
From wherever you are, hold them both up.
And hold up the trees, who don't know
where their people go or how long till
they return.

Amir & Anna

'It's unbelievable, this cycle of violence, and how neither party realises they're both losing.'
Dr Cairo Arafat, West Bank

Amir can't sleep.
He dives under his bed.
Anna is afraid of everything.
Parked cars, moving buses.
Anna is afraid of toast.
Their names begin with 'A,'
contain the same number of letters.
They live one mile apart.
No one has given them
what they deserve.
Around both their houses,
all the Arab and Jewish houses,
red poppies sleep beneath
dirt and stones.
What do they know?
In March green spokes
with fluttering heads
rise and rise on every side.

Talking Forever

for Palestine & Dareen Tatour

Say it again, resist times ten.
Those who were not politicians,
who were going to school or tending the rooms,
shops, libraries, kitchens, mint sprigs drooping in a can,
changing diapers, wiping spittle from chins,
chopping onions, snipping cucumbers from a scratchy vine,
we would have done anything for you, Palestine.
But all we knew to do was talk, talk, to everyone who already
    agreed.
Sign petitions, phone representatives, write checks,
wear *keffiyehs* tied around our necks, demonstrate,
feel hopeful that President Obama might (in his vast intelligence)
really stand up for you – what else could we do?
Talk to those who didn't already agree? But who were we?
'If they knew our stories, they wouldn't do these things to us,'
my Palestinian grandmother said, when she was 100 years old,
after being tear-gassed in her own room by Israelis.
She wasn't angry – we were.
Dareen, trapped in her house for using the word 'Resist' – she was
    there
and we were everywhere else. Easy to punish her, Israel had
no trouble trapping, oppressing, squelching, giving another name.
Pressed down for so long, those without influence over weapons or
    borders,
easy to ignore, refute, blame, always blame, changing the story,
inverting the facts... and they *did* know the story, Sitti,
because everyone told it, Dareen told it,
Mahmoud, Fadwa, Edward, Suheir, Anton, Sharif, Nathalie,
    Lisa, Lena,
Khaled, Salma, Raja, Fady, Aziz, everyone told it, kept telling it,
talking forever, but the checkpoint lines got longer, pressed,
the sad orchards smaller, looming wall more riveted with cries,
the way a nightmare compounds, spinning out swirls of

hallways, blockades, locked doors, prison cells...
the powerful kept saying, Give the oppressors more money,
they are a democracy,
and the sleeping person shouted from the nightmare, Wake up!
Just let me wake up!

Fady Joudah

Mimesis

My daughter
                       wouldn't hurt a spider
That had nested
Between her bicycle handles
For two weeks
She waited
Until it left of its own accord

If you tear down the web I said
It will simply know
This isn't a place to call home
And you'd get to go biking

She said that's how others
Become refugees isn't it?

Twice a River

After studying our faces for months
My son knows to beam
Is the thing to do

He'll spend years deciphering love
The injustice or the illusion
Having been brought into this world
Volition is an afterthought

What will I tell him
About land and language and burial
Places my father doesn't speak of
Perhaps my mother knows

In the movie the dispossessed cannot return
Even when they're dead
The journalist felt

Rebuke for not having thought
It mattered or for having thought it mattered too much

Will I tell my son all nations arise after mass
Murder that I don't know

Any national anthem by heart can't sing
'Take Me Out to the Ball Game'?

I should turn to flowers and clouds instead
Though this has already been said well
It is night

When he gazes
Into his mother's eyes at bath time
Qyss and Laila she announces after a long day's work

He giggles with his shoulders not knowing
He's installing a web

In his amygdala or whichever
Places science thinks love dwells

Even love is a place? O son
Love no country and hate none
And remember crimes sometimes

Immortalize their victims
Other times the victimizer

Remember how you used to gaze at the trampoline
Leaves on their branches?

Don't believe the sound of the sea
In a seashell believe the sea
The endless trope and don't say

Much about another's language
Learn to love it

While observing silence
For the dead and the living in it

6 Textu

Darwish

If olive trees knew the hands that had planted them
olive oil would have turned into tears!

Our names our body parts
I you

butterfly flutter
or swarm

Revenge

is not what you're after you're after what
you cannot name but names you

Revenge is after you
After you

words be my body
lick my ears against revenge

Believe

or disbelieve the massacre
took size & place it doesn't erase

the prerequisite preceding terror
Catastrophe

is not always evidence-based
Also erasure

Thank You Dark World

If not for you there'd be
among other things no poetry

no silken boredom
'only triumphal songs

of spreading happiness'
I'd like that

I Only Want From Love

That poetry makes nothing happen
nothing 2 makes poetry happen

nothing is nothing can come
of nothing comes

to mind we
are late for now

Authenticity Bargain

I love you more than the world loves itself
the world doesn't love itself that much

Eternal sameness
divided by fleeting

Algebra's
zebra

Deema K. Shehabi

Eminent Domain

A dusty doormat,
a wind that evanesces in the mouth,
a history dismembered in the body
of a sparrow crashed upon the window sill,
a flattened venison on a plate with chanterelles
in a lake resort named after a vanished tribe,
an old Damascene house with little snakes
in the holes of its cool walls,
a rust blemish on a woman's face
lit up by a surveillance flare in the dark,
a child with a lucid dream
in which he runs and jumps
over acacia trees in the Sahel,
some oleanders sheared in half in mid-blossom
in the middle of September –
an abandoned house saturated with yellow mustards
in which someone scrapes the light
at midnight and scares the children,
a ten-year-old with an M16 in Tebane
who'd rather go to school,
a conversation with my love in which he says,
Why weep at the sight of small outstretched
hands? Tomorrow, we'll go south –

Gaza Renga

From the underside
of the palm to where the sea
sutures the land, one

woman bronzes her arm,
someone's limbs tucked into lips

of her long poplar-
stitched dress. She says, 'There was smoke.'
'It was not the smoke

of a gardenless earth nor
haemorrhage of orphaned kids.'

***

This place is all we
ever grieve for – in blurred dreams,

in smoky hours, the day
light sealed from our eyes,

and nothing is ever limned:
A baby on top

of the mother's dried-up
corpse in broad daylight.

***

The oil-stained boot prints on the veil
are the same ones on the wall,

and the girl whose clothes
still smell like gas is replaced

by another with a rough voice
calling out... for what, to whom?
Balconies, buildings,

an ambulance with no driver
settle in the back of her throat.

You Are of It, More or Less Forever

I said to the boy
who asked why Abraham abandoned
Hagar to the desert.
To answer is to peer into love's irony
and not to overarm it with magnolias,
too ripe and dangerously close,
thin line of brown rot circling
white-pink blossoms, massive
in this early spring;
It is not to unpeel the boy's eyes
from first betrayals
and history's eternally bound
and fracturing tribes,
or from women who beg God
for water in deserts.
And who is to tell this boy's future
already billowing against this pavement
littered with crushed petals
or whether he will find an answer
in an encrypted fountain
and call it *Zamzam*, or love
cleared of irony,
or sign against love
that drowns in thirst,
or, if he will wonder why
his mother turned her back
on his question,
and she'll wonder
what he will call
her refusal to answer.

---

*The title, 'You are of It, More or Less Forever', is taken from Edward Said's
seminal essay on exile, 'Reflections on Exile'.*

Mahmoud Darwish

Green flies

Nothing ever changes: summers and sweat drops: and the mind can't see what's behind the horizon. Today is better than tomorrow. But the dead are still new. They're born every day. Voices are searching for words in the wilderness, and an echo comes back clear and wounding: there's no one. Still there is at least some-one who will say: It's the right of any killer to defend the instinct to kill.' And to this the dead can only respond late: 'It's the right of all victims to defend their screams.' The call of the adhan rises higher and higher over duplicate funerals: and the caskets are raised in a hurry, the burials are rushed... there's not enough time for completing the rites because now more of the dead are coming, rushing out of the raids, alone and in groups, entire families leaving no orphans or mourners behind. The sky is bullet-grey. The sea is grey-blue. But the colour of blood is already hidden from the cameras by the swarms of green flies!

Translated by Josh Calvo

Like a prosaic poem

Autumnal summer in the hills, like a prosaic poem. The breeze has a light rhythm I can feel but not hear in the humility of the bushes, and the grass is dry and yellowed, like old yellowed photos. Rhetoric tempts by metaphors and tricks of verbs. There's no celebration in this vast expanse but the flight of the sparrows between meaning and meaninglessness. Nature is a body casting off cheap ornamentations, while its figs, grapes, and pomegranates wait to ripen, and forgotten lusts are reawakened by the rains. 'Were it not for this inscrutable need of mine for poetry, I would not need anything at all,' argues the poet whose dulled enthusiasm has lessened his mistakes. He walks because the doctors have recommended he take these aimless walks that will retrain his heart to maintain that indifference so necessary for health. If he thinks of some idea it's only ever random and fleeting. The summer will rarely be fit to chant in verse. The summer is a prosaic poem indifferent to the eagles circling above.

Translated by Josh Calvo

Beyond my identity

I'm sitting in front of the TV because I don't have the strength to do anything else. Here in front of the TV I'll discover my passion. I'll see what's happening in me, to me. Smoke rises up around me while I try to clutch hold of my fingers, chopped-off and scattered among the endless bodies, but I don't find them and I don't run from them because the pain is too compelling. I am besieged by land sky sea and language. The last plane has taken off from the airport in Beirut to drop me in front of this TV, so that I can watch the rest of my death along with millions of other viewers. Nothing will prove I exist, if I think like Descartes, except the smoke of myself rising from a sacrifice brought in Lebanon. I enter the TV along with the monster. I know the monster is stronger than me in the struggle of the planes against the birds, but I've become more attached to the bravery of the metaphor than I should be: the monster has swallowed but not yet digested me. I emerge untouched more than once. My soul has flown up out of me and the monster's belly to inhabit another body, lighter but stronger than ours. I don't know where I am: in front of the TV or inside it. But now I can see my heart tumbling like a pinecone down from the mountains of Lebanon, toward Gaza!

Translated by Josh Calvo

Nero

What's bouncing around Nero's brain while he watches Lebanon burn? With his darting eyes, drunk, traipsing around like he's dancing at a wedding: this madness is my madness, dear sirs of philosophy: so why shouldn't they burn it all, burn everything but what I command! And let the children learn to mind their manners, to be seen and not heard screaming while I'm making my music!

What's bouncing around Nero's brain while he watches Iraq burn? Is he happy enough knowing he's stirred up a memory in the history of the forests, knowing his name is inscribed as an enemy of Hammurabi and Gilgamesh and Abu Nuwas? My law is the mother of all laws! And the flower of immortality is sown in my fields! But poetry – what could that word mean?

What's bouncing around Nero's brain while he watches Palestine burn? Does it delight him to hear his name rolled out among the annals of the Prophets, like the name of a Prophet no one ever believed in: a Prophet of killing entrusted by God to correct those endless errors recorded in heavenly tomes: 'I, too, am the spokesman of God!'

What's bouncing around Nero's brain while he watches the world burn? I am Lord of the Resurrection. But then he orders the camera to stop rolling, so that no one will see his fingers in flames at the end of this long American movie!

Translated by Josh Calvo

Sara Saleh

oud

You tell me you're not really into *oud*
When I have dedicated my life to mastery of us
It takes discipline, I say
They tried to call it theirs,
But it is part of my body
The *oud* cannot give you anything unless you give of yourself
You give and you spend time
And you hold it
You have to hold it well
For it to share its secrets.

Nobody likes to remember the death that walked the streets with us.
We never stop playing, as though if we do, we will forget.
We never stop playing, maybe that means we have lost.

to the cities that changed us

Sydney 1995

i went missing with you
especially in times when i couldn't find myself

i will miss biting your fairyfloss sky
holding on tight to your tired old swing sets,
the way children's hands should be held on Sundays.

in transit 1996

it would take me twenty years
to let myself come back to this point
to you.

Beirut 1999

you were a window in time
i wish they'd stop calling you
the 'Paris of the Middle East'
it's violating.

Dubai 2001

the hungry decided to ring the dinner bell
everything changed.

we went to the warehouses, we found our flesh
at stocktake.

Beirut 2005

you realised all you'll ever be is
a piece…
and you were ok with that.
you will be the one piece that counts.

Prague 2006

you are a treasure hunt but i am clueless
i still open up what's left of my chest to you
and palm you like a prayer.

London 2007

temptation never had my back, i fall back into lonely.

Sydney 2009

nothing comes with an exit strategy
nine-to-five is playtime but you raise strong sons and daughters
as though we aren't trying to educate our families
in the ways of making peace with their own blood
and beliefs
we pack away confusion in boxes
we stack them in the corner.

Sydney 2012

you are open for profit but
closed for people.

i scratch at my name
standing in lines
so they learn how to say ours
so their throats are homes
for Ali
for Ahmad
for Mohamed

nothing beats feeling free
...even in darkness.

Jerusalem 2013

you say little to me,
and little sounds like heartbreak.
little sounds like protection.
i am not ready for your wounds and your truths.
you come back to me like consolation.

Sydney 2014

your graceful fingers wrote
the history of your people
the way spiders
spin their silken webs
of survival.

Cairo 2014

you have the burial rites
to everyone I have ever
found home in.

New York, New Year's Eve

the only museum I want to
discover is him
find me a flashlight...
he is all art and history
and a fist full of fireworks
he reminds me how to sing,
again.

Sydney 2015

in the moments you breathe me in
that is where
my world ends.
and begins.

the seas 2015

we are found in dirty spots of our fluid
between loin and ribs
our end in dirty spots of this earth
between road and rot

how do we walk through this life
demanding ours matters
more than others?

there are sea cemeteries that have seen
more heart than us.

Melbourne 2015

we weren't quite ourselves.
or maybe we'd never been
more ourselves.

and we danced.
we always knew how
to dance.

Sydney 2016

how sad it is
you are filled with universes
that will never touch again

you and i
are cities in yearning.

شفرة العشب:
مختارات من الشعر الفلسطيني الجديد

شفرة العشب:
مختارات من الشعر الفلسطيني الجديد
تحرير نعومي فويل

المحتويات

المشاركون

مايا أبو الحيات شاعرة وروائية وممثلة وكاتبة للأطفال ومديرة ورشة فلسطين للكتابة في بيرزيت. ألفت ثلاثة دواوين شعرية، وحصلت على جائزة مؤسسة عبد المحسن القطان للشعراء الشباب. ولدت في لبنان عام ١٩٨٠، وهي مقيمة حاليا في القدس مع زوجها وأولادها.

مصطفى أبو سنينة شاعر وكاتب من مدينة القدس. صدر ديوانه الشعري الأوّل *غيمة سوداء في نهاية السطر* عام ٢٠١٦. درس القانون في جامعة بيرزيت، وحصل على درجة الماجستير في الدراسات الاستعمارية من كلية غولدسميث في جامعة لندن.

وليد البزون محاضر في الأدب الإنكليزي في جامعة البصرة في العراق. حاصل على شهادة الدكتوراه في الأدب القصصي المعاصر من جامعة تشيشستر حيث درس في قسم الأدب الإنكليزي والكتابة الابداعية. نشرت مجموعتة الشعرية *الحرب على دجلة* عام ٢٠١١.

فاتنة الغرة ولدت وتعلمت في غزة، حيث عملت في مشاريع النساء والصحافة. ألفت ثلاث دواوين وكانت مشاركة في ورشة آيوا للكتابة.

طارق الحيدر كاتب تم نشر أعماله في مجلات مثل *ثريبيني ريفيو* و*نورث أمريكان ريفيو* و*داياغرام* وغيرها. كما تم إدراج إحدى مقالاته ضمن الأعمال الجديرة بالذكر في *أفضل المقالات الأمريكية ٢٠١٦*.

فريد سليم البيطار شاعر أمريكي فلسطيني، ولد في القدس عام ١٩٦١. حرّر أنثولوجيا شعرية اسمها *مختارات من الحب العربي* ٢٠٠٩ وألف دواوين شعرية منها *خطوات في الضباب* وأصدر ألبومين اسمهما *فتوش* و*شتات*. سيصدر ديوانه القادم *خطوط ضبابية – ٤٨|٦٧*، عام ٢٠١٨.

جوش كلفو طالب للدكتوراه في قسم الأدب المقارن في جامعة برينستن في نيو جرزي، حيث يعمل على الأدب العربي والعبري في العصر الحديث. أصله يهودي سوري، وكذلك نشأ على المزيج بين الثقافة العربية واليهودية. من خارج

أعماله الأكاديمية، يكتب كلفو قصص قصيرة وروايات أصيلة ويترجم الكتب المحبوبة عليه.

رفاييل كوهين مواطن بريطاني أقام وعمل في القاهرة منذ منعه من الدخول إلى إسرائيل في عام ٢٠٠٦. هو مترجم ومعجمي مع اهتمام باللسانيات الحاسوبية. من ترجماته المنشورة *أحدّثك لكيّ ترى* لمنى برنس، و*ذاكرة الجسد* لأحلام مستغانمي، و*أجنحة الفراشة* لمحمد سلماوي.

ولد **محمود درويش (١٩٤١-٢٠٠٨)** في قرية البروة في منطقة الجليل الفلسطيني، لكنه عاش طوال حياته في عدة مدن، ومنها بيروت، ورام الله، وتونس، وباريس، وغيرها. أنه واحد من الشعراء المحبوبين والمعروفين في العالم العربي، ونشر أكثر من ٣٠ ديوان شعري، أغلبيتها ترجمت الى ٣٥ لغات عالمية. تقديرا لفنّه العريق، كرّم درويش بوسام الفنون والآداب الفرنسي وحصل على جائزة اللنان للحرية الثقفية عام ٢٠٠١، وجائزة الأمير كلاوس عام ٢٠٠٤، وجائزة القاهرة للشعر العربي عام ٢٠٠٧.

ولد الفنان والشاعر **أشرف فياض** سنة ١٩٨٠ في المملكة العربية السعودية لعائلة لاجئة من غزة. رعى معارض للفن السعودي في أوروبا وفي المملكة العربية السعودية. في عام ٢٠١٦ وبسبب قصائد في مجموعته الشعرية *الأوامر من الداخل*، تم اتهامه بالردة وحكم عليه بالموت وبعد مراجعة الحكم تم سجنه لثمان سنوات مع ٨٠٠ جلدة. سوف تصدر مجموعته الثانية المكتوبة بالسجن بعنوان *تاريخ مرضي* قريبا.

نعومي فويل شاعرة وروائية وكاتبة مسرح شعري وكاتبة مقالة ومحررة. من ضمن كتبها العديدة: *جناح الليل،* توصية مجمع الشعر في خريف ٢٠٠٨، *تاريخ غايا،* رباعيات خيالية علمية وقد ترجمت بالمشاركة مع رائد خنجر قصيدة *جراح الغيمة،* تعيش في برايتن وتدرّس الكتابة الابداعية في جامعة تشيشيستر.

كاثرين هولز مترجمة مستقلة متخصصة في المسرح والسينما. صدرت ترجمتها مع آدم طالب لرواية رجاء عالم *طوق الحمام* الحائزة على البوكر العربي عام ٢٠١١.

فادي جودة شاعر ومترجم وطبيب مقيم في هيوستن. حصلت أعماله الأدبية على عدة جوائز أمريكية، كندية، وبريطانية. له أربعة دواوين شعرية وخمسة في الترجمة.

ولد **بلال خالد** في خان يونس في غزة عام ١٩٩٢، وهو خطاط ورسام الغرافيتي الجداريات ومصور صحافي. مقيم حاليا في تركيا فإنه يعمل دوليا، وتظهر أعماله في عدة منافذ إعلامية، منها النيويورك تايمز، الغارديان، والجزيرة.

أندرو ليبر طالب للدكتوراه في قسم العلوم السياسية في جامعة هارفارد. صدرت ترجماته في عدة منشورات بالإضافة لتحريره لمجموعات من الأدب العراقي والسوداني.

سارة ماغير مؤسسة ومديرة مركز ترجمة الشعر ومؤلفة اربع مجاميع شعرية تتضمن *رمان قندهار* وهو اختيار المجمع الشعري وعد ضمن القائمة القصيرة لجائزة توماس ستيرنز ايليت سنة ٢٠٠٧. حصلت على جائزة تشلمندلي.

آنا مورسن حاصلة على شهادة الماجستير في اللغة العربية من كلية الدراسات الاسيوية والافريقية وحاصلة على شهادة البكلوريوس في اللغة العربية من جامعة إدنبرة، وهي متخصصة في الشعر العراقي الحديث.

ولد **مروان مخول** عام ١٩٧٩ في قرية البقيعة في أعالي الجليل لأب فلسطيني وأم لبنانية. كمواطن فلسطيني مسيحي في إسرائيل، شعره يعكس هوية معقدة وفخر شديد كشاعر عربي. نشر عدد من الدواوين وأعمال إبداعية أخرى وحصد العديد من الجوائز الأولى تقديرًا له على أعماله الأدبيّة، على مستوى فِلَسطين والعالم العربيّ.

سارة صالح ناشطة وكاتبة عربية أسترالية تعمل في مجال المساعدة الإنسانية وحقوق الإنسان. بالإضافة الى كونها شريكة مؤسس الصلام الشعري في دبي، وصلت صالح الى المرحلة النهائية في الصلام الشعري الدولي الأسترالي، ومثلت شعريا دوليا ووطنيا. صدر ديوانها الشعري أغسطس الماضي.

وجدان شمالة فلسطينية نيوزيلاندية عاملة من أجل مجتمعات اللاجئين في أوستراليا. درست في أقسام العلاقات الدولية والتعلم والتطور.

ديمة ك. شهابي شاعرة وكاتبة ومحررة نشرت في أماكن عديدة. نشأت في العالم العربي والتحقت بجامعة في الولايات المتحدة، حيث حصلت على شهادة الماجستير في الصحافة. تتبعت ديوانها الأول، *ثلاث عشر مغادرات من القمر*، بعمل اشتراكي مع مارلين هاكر، اسمه *شتات/رنغا*.

نعومي شهاب ناي شاعرة أميركية فلسطينية مقيمة في ولاية تكساس. ولدت في سانت لويس وعاشت في القدس في شبابها. كتبت وحررت أكثر من ٣٠ ديوان شعري وكتابات نثرية للقراء الشباب والبالغين ومنها: *حبيبي، أسرار جدتي، تسعة عشر نوع من الغزلان، وسلحفاة عمان.*

أحمد طه عبد ربه شاعر من أبرز شعراء السبعينيات في مصر ومؤسس جماعة أصوات الشعرية. أصدر مجلة *الكتابة السوداء* عام ١٩٨٨ التي اهتمت بالتيارات الجديدة في الفكر والشعر وفي ١٩٩٤ أصدر أيضا مجلة *الجراد* وهي التي دشنت جيل التسعينيات في الشعر المصري. من دواوينه الشعرية *الطاولة ٤٨، وإمبراطورية الحوائط، وممر البستان.*

دارين طاطور شاعرة و مصورة من قرية الرينة في الجليل. تتحدى قصائدها الثورية الاحتلال والظلم الإجتماعي و مصير النساء. تم اعتقالها بتهمة التحريض في شهر أكتوبر ٢٠١٥ بسبب قصيدة كتبتها، وهي لا تزال تحت الإقامة الجبرية في منزلها لحين انتهاء محاكمتها. أثارت قضية دارين الاستنكار و الاستهجان في العالم أجمع.

إلى آية وكونور واسكندر
فريدة ووجد ومنى وزياد
اليافعين المنطلقين إلى الحياة

إلى أرواح محمود درويش (١٩٤٢-٢٠٠٨)
ومحمود أبو سمرة (٢٠٠٠-٢٠٠٨)

مروان مخول

عربي في مطار بن غوريون

أنا عربي!
صحتُ في باب المطار
فاختصرتُ لجنديّةِ الأمنِ الطّريقَ إليّ،
ذهبتُ إليها وقلتُ: استجوبيني، ولكن
سريعًا، لو سمحتِ، لأنّي لا أريد التّأخّرَ
عن موعد الطّائرة.
قالت: من أين أنت؟
من غساسنةِ الجَولان أصلُ فروسيّتي ـ قلتُ
جارُ مومسٍ من أريحا؛
تلك الّتي وشّتْ إلى يهوذا بالطّريقِ إلى الضّفّة الغربيّة
يوم احتلّها فاحتلّها التّاريخُ من بعدهِ
في الصّفحة الأولى.
من حَجر الخليل الصُّلبِ أجوبتي
وُلدتُ زمنَ المؤابيّينَ النّازلينَ من قبلكم
أرضَ الزّمانِ الخانعة،
من كنعانَ أبي
وأمّي فينيقيّةٌ من جنوب لبنان في السّابقْ،
ماتت أمُّها، أمّي، قبل شهرين
ولم توذّعْ جثمانَ أمّها، أمّي، قبل شهرين،
بكيتُ بحضنها كي تؤانسَها الألفةُ في البُقَيعَةِ
عند سفح المُصيبة والنّصيب،
لبنانُ يا أختُ المستحيلْ، وأنا
أمُّ أمّي الوحيدةُ
في الشّمال!

سألتني: ومن رتَّبَ الحقيبةَ لك؟
قلتُ: أسامة بنُ لادن، ولكن!
رويدكِ، فهذا مُزاحُ الجِراح المتاحُ،
نكتةٌ يحترفُها الواقعيّونَ مثلي ها هنا
في الكفاحْ،
أناضلُ منذ ستّينَ عامًا بالكلام عن السّلام،
لا أسطو على المستوطنة،
ولستُ أملِكُ مثلَكُم دبّابةً كالّتي
على متنها، دغدغَ الجنديُّ غزّة،
لم أرمِ قنبلةً من الأباتشي في سِجلّيَ الشّخصيُّ
لا لنقص فيّ
بل لأنّيَ أرى في الأفقِ المدى صدى السّأمِ
من ثورةِ السّلميِّ في غير موضعها
ومن حُسن السّلوك.

***

هل أعطاكَ أحدُهُم شيئًا في الطّريق إلى هنا ـ سألت،
قلتُ: هو المنفيُّ في النّيربْ
أعطانيَ الذّكرياتْ
ومِفتاحَ بيتٍ في الحكاياتْ
صدأ الحديدِ على المفتاح وتَّرَني ولكنّي
كالمَعدِن الأصليِّ؛ أُرجِّعُ ذاتي بذاتي، إن أحنّ،
من أنين اللاجئينْ
يَبعثُ الشّوقُ جناحهُ عبر الحدودِ
لا حَرسٌ أو ألفُ يمنعُهُ
ولا أنتِ، أكيد.

***

قالت: هل من أداةٍ حادّةٍ في حيازتكَ؟
قلتُ: عاطفت

بَشَرتي.. وملامحُ القمحيِّ فيَّ،
وُلدتُ هنا بلا ذنبٍ سوى الحظِّ،
متشائلًا قد كنتُ في السَّبعين
أنا المتفائلَ بأنشودتين عصيّتين عليكِ الآن
في سجنِ جِلْبُوَعْ.
أَصلي
وفصلي من رواياتِ الزَّمانِ الفجِّ
جنازةُ الماضي وعرسٌ
في قاعةِ الأملِ القريب،
بلحٌ من الغَورِ رعرعني
وفسَّرني الكلام.
في حيازتي طفلٌ أجَّلتُه عن موعد التَّوليدِ كي يأتي
إلى صباحٍ لا كهذا الهشِّ يا بنت أوكرانيا.
في حيازتّي أنَّ المؤذِّنَ صادحًا يُطربُني رغم الحادي
أصيخُ كي تَجفُلَ الأُنّاثُ في النّاياتْ
وكي تَصدَحَ الكمنجةُ في الطَّبنجةِ من خلودٍ في الوجود.

***

تأخذني الجنديّةُ إلى تفتيشِ حاجاتي
تأمرُني بفتح الحقيبة،
أفعلُ ما تشاء!
فينزُّ من قلب الحقيبة قلبي، وأغنيتي
ومعنى المعنى يُزُّ فصاحةً وفجاجةً منها وفيها كلُّ ما فيَّ.

***

تسألني: وما هذا؟
أقولُ: سورةُ الإسراءِ من معراج أوردتي وتفسيرُ الجلالين،
ديوانُ أبي الطيِّب المتنبّي وأختي مرام، صورةً وحقيقةً في آن،
شالٌ حريريٌّ يدثِّرني ويحميني من بردِ البُعادِ عن الأقاربْ،
تَبغٌ من عرّابة البطَوفِ دوَّخَني إلى أن حشّشَ المجهولَ فيَّ
وفيَّ وفيٌّ وفيٌّ.. زعترٌ بلديٌّ
جلَّنارُ النّارْ، جليليٌّ بَهيٌّ

عقيقي، كافوري، بَخورُي وأنّيَ حَيٌّ.
مَرجانُ حيفا المِشعُّ المستديمُ المستنيرُ
المستحيلُ المستريحُ في جيبِ عودتِنا بلا سببٍ
سوى أنّا عَبَدنا حُسنَ نِيّتِنا وأوثَقَنا
النّكبةُ السقطةُ في الماضي وفيّ!

***

تُسَلِّمُني الجنديّةُ إلى الشّرطيِّ الّذي
تحسّسني في فجأةٍ ثمّ صاح:
ما هذا؟!
عضويَ الوطنيُّ - أقولُ
ونسلي.. حمى أهلي وبيضتا حمامٍ
تفقسانِ رجولةً وأنوثةً منّي ولي،
يبحثُ بي
عن كلّ شيءٍ ممكنٍ وخطيرْ
لكنّهُ أعمى هذا الغريبَ الّذي
ينسى قنابلَ بي أشدَّ مضاضةً وأهمّ:
عنفواني، جُموحي، نزقَ النّسور في لهفي وفي جسدي
شَهامَتي وشهامتي، هذا أنا
كاملًا متكاملًا لن يراني فيما يرى
هذا الغبيّ.

***

الآنَ، وبعد ساعتينِ من معركة المعنويّاتْ
ألعقُ جرحي لخمسِ دقائقَ كافياتْ
ثمّ أصعدُ الطّائرة الّتي ارتفعت. لا للذَّهاب
ولا للإياب،
بل لأرى جنديّةَ الأمنِ تحتي
الشّرطيَّ في نشيدِ حذائيَ الوطنيِّ تحتي
وتحتي أكذوبة التّاريخ المعلّبِ مِثلَ
بن غوريون الّذي صارَ كما كان كما كان
تحتي.

مسائيّة

مساؤك ليلٌ مُحلّى
أيا مَن كقطر النّدى
من على شجر الرَّنْد نزّتْ عليّ؛
لأصحو مع الفجر أنفُضُهُ
قبل أن يفتحَ الصّبحُ عينَهُ أو يتلوّى.

مساؤكِ مَنٌّ وسلوى
وجمرٌ يُؤجَّجُ تحتَ هشيمِ المشاعِرْ
فأنتِ اللّهيبُ
وجسميَ فوقَكِ لانَ قُبيلَ يذوبُ،
فهل تسمحينَ ليَ، الآنَ، أن أرثي نفسي
وأن أَتَشظّى؟

مساؤكِ فتوى
وربٌّ رؤوفٌ يَعِزُّ عليّ
فأغدو التّقيَّ الّذي حجَّ
منكِ إليكِ وصلّى.

مساؤكِ مأوى
ونهرٌ من المِسكِ صُبَّ عليّ
كأنّيَ للنّهر عشبٌ يميلُ عليهِ
ليشرَبَ منهُ ويُروى

تعالَي نُحاولْ عُبورَ المسافة
ما بينَ قطبينِ منفصلينِ بخَيلِ الغريزةِ،
أو نَجْسُر البعدَ يا سِدرةَ المنتهى!
حيثُ لا بُدَّ للحظِّ أن يَتَثنّى إلينا
وأن يتجلّى.

تعالَى إليَّ!
لأنَّ الفِراقَ خبيئًا يُطلُّ علينا
تعالَي! ليُغمى عليهِ الفِراقُ ويُنسى
تعالَي فيُنسى.

مساؤكِ ذنبٌ وأدهى
توهَّزَ فوقَ غزالةٍ روحي على النّبعِ
كانَت تحدّقُ في حُسنها
كي تُجمِّلَ من شكلِها في مرايا المياهِ
لتبدوَ أجلى فأحلى

مساؤكِ ذنبٌ وأغبى
فلو في الهجوم تريّثَ شيئًا
لقبَّلَ وجه الفريسةِ
ثُمَّ تذوّقَ ما صارَ بعد التَّأنّي
غزالًا لذيذًا.. وأشهى.

في قطار تل أبيب

في القطار إلى تل أبيب
رأيتُها.. روسيّةً،
تَدلُّ إلى مَنبع النعناع.
كان بحوزتها موسكو كلُّها
وطفلٌ كما يبدو
شرقي

في المقصورة ذاتِها أثيوبيٌّ
حَدَّقَ في وجوه المسافرين،
حَدَّقَ.. إلى أن ملَّهُم
فراح ينظر من النافذة
إلى حُطامِ قريةٍ لا تَعنيـة

عاملٌ من القادمين الجدد
نشيطٌ، بعدَ قليل سينزلُ
من القطار إلى عمله في شركةٍ
أعلنت للتو عن طَرده

على يميني جلسَ يهوديٌّ
مغربيّ، حَدَّثني عن أحواله
إلى أن اكتشف لُكْنَتي،
هوَ تابعَ حديثَهُ ولكن
مع الذي على يمينه

بعدها.. وفي أقرب محطّة نزلتُ
لأنَّ القصيدة انتهت

دارين طاطور

قاوم يا شعبي قاومهم

في القدس ضَمَّدْتُ جراحي
وَنَفَثْتُ همومي لِله
وحملت الروح على كفّي
من أجل فلسطين عربية
لن أرضى بالحل السلمي
لن أنزل أبَدًا راياتي
حتى أنْزِلهُمْ منْ وطني
أُركِعُهم لِزَمانٍ آت
قاوم يا شعبي قاومهم
قاوم سطو المستوطن
واتبع قافلة الشهداءِ
مزِّق دستورا من عارٍ
قد حَملَ الذّلَ القهَّارِ
أرْدَعَنا مِنْ رَدِّ الحَق
حرقوا الأطفال بلا ذنبٍ
وَهديلَ قنصوها عَلنًا
قتلوها في وَضَح نهار
قاوم يا شعبي قاومهم
قاوم بطش المستعمر
لا تصغ السمع لأذنابٍ
ربطونا بالوهم السلمي
لا تخشى السُنَ مرتابة
فالحقُ في قَلْبِكَ أقْوى
ما دُمتَ تُقَاوم في وطنٍ
عاش الغزوات وما كلَّ
فعليُ نادى من قبره
قاوم يا شعبي الثائر

واكتبني نثرًا في النذ
قد صِرتَ الردَّ لأشلائي
قاوم يا شعبي قاومهم

شاعرة من وراء القضبان

في السجن قابلت أناسًا
لا رقم لها بل لا تحصى...
وهناك القاتل والجاني...
وهناك السارق والكاذب...
وهناك الصادق والكافر...
وهناك الضائع والحائر...
وهناك المجرم والجائع...
وهناك المرضى بالوطن
قد جاؤوا من رحم الألم
عاشوا مع كل الظلم...
حتى أن صاروا أطفالاً واغتصبت كل براءتهم
وانصدموا من قهر الدنيا
كبروا...
بل كبرت احزانًا...
قد عظمت مع كل الكبت...
كالورد في تربة ملح
واعتنقوا الحب بلا خوفٍ...
وكان الذنب إذ قالوا
نحب الوطن بلا حدٍّ...
ما عرفوا ابدًا ما فعلوا...
فصار العشق جريمتهم
والسجن مصير العشاق
وبدأت أحاور في روحي
في لحظة شكٍّ وشرودي
ماذا عن جرمك يا نفسي
لا أعرف معناه الآن...!؟
الشيء الواحد قد قلته
أني أفصحت بأفكاري
فكتبت عن الظلم الجاري...
خططت بحبري أهاتي...
بقصيدة شعر أكتبها...
التهمة قد لبست جسدي

من اخمص قدمي للرأسِ
فأنا شاعرة في السجن
شاعرة من بلد الفن
كلماتي التهمة في الحكم
القلم أداة الاجرام
الحبر دماء الاحساس جعلوه الباصم الشاهد
من أجل النطق بتهمتنا...
إسمع يا قدري ياعمري
ما قال الحاكم والقاضي
فقصيدتي صارت متهمة
وقصيدتي صارت إجرامٌ
في بلد الحكم ـ الحرية ـ
السجن مصير الفنان.....!!!

٢٠١٥|١١|٢

سجن الجلمة
اليوم الذي قُدمت لي فيه لائحة الاتهام

أنا مَنْ أكون؟

الرِّيحُ تَسْأَلُ مَن أنا..!
أَنْتَ الأَنا
يا صَوْتِيَ إنِّي أنا أُنْثى الرَّحيلْ
المَذعورَ في لَيْلِ الضَّبابْ
أوْ فاكْتُبي أُنْثى الـمُحالْ
أَبْقى أَسيرٌ بِلا انْحناءْ
أَرْضى بِعَيْشِ اللَّا مَكانْ
أَمْضي وَطَيْفي لَيْسَ يَعْنيهِ البَقاءْ
حُرِّيَّتي...
صَوْتُ النِّساءْ

وَالبَحْرُ يَسْأَلُ مَنْ أَنا؟
أَنَا دُرُّهُ الـمَدْفونُ في قَلْبِ الغُموضْ
وَالصَّبْرُ في رَمْلِ الزَّمانْ
إنِّي أنا..
إعْصارُ مَوْجٍ غاضِبٍ وَقْتَ الغُروبْ
إذْ عانَقَتْ أَنْفاسُهُ حِضْنَ الرِّياحْ
أَدْنو وَيَسْلُبُني السُّؤالْ
وَبَقيتُ أَسْأَلُ مَنْ أكونْ؟

وَطَنٌ وَيَسْأَلُ مَنْ أنا؟
إنِّي هُنا
وَخُلِقْتُ مِنْ رَحِمِ الشَّقاءْ
طِفْلًا يُحاصِرُهُ الأَلَمْ
دَمْعًا يُكَبِّلُهُ الغَضَبْ
إنِّي أَنا عِشْقُ الوَطَنْ
قَدْ عِشْتُ في هْذا البَلَدْ
وَكَبُرْتُ في شِرْيانِ ناصِرَةٍ
غَدَّتْ لِميلادِ الـمُنى لَحْنَ السَّلامْ
وَبَقيتُ صامِدَةً هُنا
أَبْني لَها حُلُمَ الأَبَدْ

٢٤

والنَّخْلُ يَسْأَلُ مَنْ أَنا؟
أَنا مِثْلُهُ
لِلشَّمْسِ شامِخَةً بَقِيتْ
أَعْلو وَظِلِّي واقِفٌ
فَوْقَ الجَبِينِ وَلَنْ أَموتْ
إِلَّا وَجِذْعي نازِعٌ مِنْ صَرْخَتي
حَرْفَ السُّكوتْ

وَالنَّفْسُ تَسْأَلُ مَنْ أَنا
إِنِّي أَنا بَوْحُ الضَّميرْ
إِنْسانَةٌ تُبْدي السُّؤالْ
هَلْ ما أُعايِشُ واقِعٌ؟
أَمْ أَنَّهُ وَحْيُ الخَيالْ
حَيْرى أَنا في عالَمٍ باعَ الأَمانْ
قَدْ صارَ يَحْجُبُهُ اليَبابْ
وَابْتاعَ أَلْوانَ الضَّبابْ
يا عُمْرُ فاشْرَبْ وَارْتَوِ
سَيَظَلُّ يُحْيينا السَّحابْ

مايا أبو الحيات

أنا امرأة معدمة

أعيش على حاجز
أفرح لأشياء تافهة
كأن يمر يومي دون رؤية جندي واحد
يشعر بالملل
أكتب روايتي الجديدة هناك
عن الدباح الذي أراد أن يصبح عازف كمان
سيء وفاحش
لكن يده خذلته
لصالح سكين حادة وتلمع
أنت تعلم كم هو كئيب
أن تكون معدماً وتعيش على حاجز
وتفرح لأشياء بسيطة
كأن تتخطى شاعراً ثرثاراً
وعمالاً متعبين يحملون أكياساً
من الموز والجوافا وحليب تنوفا
أنا امرأة معدمة
أعيش في قبر منذ سنين
حتى الآن
لم أر شياطين أو ملائكة
لكنني رأيت الكثير من الجنود النعسين

صور مؤلمة

سأخبرك عن الصور المؤلمة
في البرد،

١

عشرون رجلاً
بمعاطف جلدية كالحة
وجزم ومشّايات وأبواط رياضية رخيصة
وجوه تطلق اللحى والوجع والبرد
أفواه تلتف بأيدٍ وحطّات وأوشحة
ثلج يسقط على كل شيء
وتقول الجملة في الأسفل:
"سوريون ينتظرون في البرد والمطر دَورهم لِيَشتروا الخبز"
ودعوة لمشاهدة المزيد،
لا أدخل لأرى
لست نبيّة على أية حال
لست إلا شخصاً يشعر بالملل
ويقلب الصور المؤلمة
ليبكي قليلاً ويشكر الله
على نعمة البيت الدافئ
ثم يضع المزيد من الخرق على النافذة
ليسكت الصفير

٢

"المزيد من الصور المؤلمة انقر هنا"

تبصّر

أنتظر ابنة شهيد شجاعة
تقف في وجهنا وتصرخ
خذوا أوطانكم
وأعيدوا لي أبي

يعرف النوار أن عمره قصيراً
لكنه يشق البرعم ويزهر
وفقط حين يتساقط على شارع المدارس
يحدث الفرح

كل دقائق الصمت
لن تعيد صوتاً واحداً إلى الحياة

عشت حياة مليئة بالرائعين
والأنذال
الآن لم أعد قادرة على التمييز بينهم

لقد رأيت أطفالاً
يمنحون آباءهم للوطن
لكنني لم أر وطناً
يمنح يتيماً أباً

أريد أن يحيا الجميع ولا يسقط أحد
ولا حتى أفكاري السيئة
ولا حتى أفكارك السيئة
ربما إن لم يسقط أحد منا
علونا كلنا دفعة واحدة
فوق هذا الجحيم

صفير

هل ترون الفجوة التي في عنقي
لم أعد أذكر إن كانت من فعل رصاصة أو كلمة
لكنني أكيدة أن شفتين مرّتا من هناك
تركتا في الفجوة صفيراً
لهذا تسمعون هذه الخشخشة
كلما تلفتُّ إلى الوراء
أو تطلعت إلى المستقبل

لا أصدق الحزن المشاع

ولا الحب في العلن
لا أصدق حديث العدالة لمدة طويلة
ولا حديث القناعة أيضاً
إن لم تكن شريراً بعض الشيء
سأعرف أنك شرير جداً
بعض الأشياء
لا يمكن تصديقها

فاتنة الغرة

زِرٌّ مَفقودْ

تبدو شَاحبة هذا الصباح
المارَّة يذهَبون بَعيداً عن الفَساتينَ الملوَّنَة
تصْطَفُّ المرايا على الرَّصيفِ تَنْتَظِرُ وجوهاً
لا وجوه تفتَرِشُ الطُّرقَاتِ بعد
يغزو الوسَنُ أكفَّ المارَةِ المتلاصقة
وحده قميص وحيد
يبدو على الدَّربِ فاغراً فاه للمدى
أي شوك رماك في درب المرايا؟
ينهض الصَّباح عن جُفونٍ مُثقَلةٍ بالدائرين حَول اللاشيء

وحده القَميصُ من يعْرِفُ وجْهَهم
وحده
ووحدهم يغتَرِفونَ اللذة القادمة من تفاصيل المساومة
يغرق في الترقب لآتٍ لم يعرف ثمناً لشيء
لم يعرف كيف يمتص الشبقَ من زرٍّ مَفقودْ
في النصفِ المختفي وراء الرقم المدوَّن في الفَراغ البعيد
يتَلمسُ الزرُّ نفسَه ويطلِقُ تنهداته

حين عبرَتْ يدُها الواجهةَ الزجاجيَّةَ واكتشفَتْ غيابَه
تلاشَتْ صورُ العابرين في عَتْمَةِ غيبتها الطرية
هي الطراوة دائماً سرَّ التوهج المتَسَاقِطِ في الواجِهَةِ الزُّجَاجِيَّةِ.

أنا غريمتك

أنا غريمتك
جرب أن تفتح فاهًا تجاهي
كي تخرج كل الثقوب السوداء من جوفي
تفتح لي بابًا وتغلقه بهذه القسوة
ترخي قلاعك وتفتح أشرعتك للأدعية
وتقف حائرًا أمام دعائي اليتيم
أنا غريمتك
المطالبة السائلة العاتية الرافضة
خائبة الأمل المذنبة المتعَبة المتعِبة
لديك حججك
بأنني ساذجة وأن عينيّ ما زالتا صغيرتين على الرؤية
أعلم هذه الإجابة جيدًا وجاهزة لها بدفاعاتي
أريد جناحيّ
وأنت لا تكف عن التدخل وليّ ذارعي وفرش طريقي بالشراك

حسنًا
لا مشكلة لدي في ذلك
غير أن وعودك الدائمة لي
ـبأن هذا العبث سيتوقف يومًا ماـ
لم تتحقق
أنا غريمتك المفتّتة من الداخل
مثل قطعة كريستال تم لصقها بعد تكسّرها

البكّاءة ذات الصوت المرتفع والضحكة مترامية الأطراف
آتيك مدججة بحججي الدامغة
ووسائل اتهامي التي لن تصمد أمامها
غريمتك تقبع الآن
في زاوية معتمة ترقب الطريق
بأنفاس متقطّعة قوية تكاد تخلع هذا القلب المثخن
أنتظر اللحظة التي أتأكد فيها من خلوّ الطريق من المارة
لأخرج وأعوي

أعوي في وجهك وعليك وأعوي على الحياة
تلك الكلبة
لن أتوقف عن العواء
عن ركل الهواء والشتائم المقذعة
حتى تطل عليّ وتخبرني
لماذا عجنت قلبي في هذا الإناء المخروم
وتركت كل هذه الفتحات تنخر فيه
كمعبر لتهريب البضائع التالفة
لن أتوقف عن العواء
وأنت تجيب بأن العجين كان طريًا أكثر مما ظننت
وأن العناصر لم تكتمل
لذلك شكلته ببعض الطين وعشب الشتاء الطري
كلما أوشك على الجفاف
نزّ هذا العشب ماءه

دم

أحمر كما ينبغي أن يكون
متدفقٌ هكذا
يحفر في روحي مكانًا للصراخ
يتدفق كأنه انفجار مخلّفًا أشلاء
يواصل تدفقه بلا ملل أو تسامح
يأخذ جانبًا من روحي
عندما تزلزل صرخته جسدي
أحمر تمامًا
لا يهادن في اللّون ولا في نوع الألم
يشقّ طريقه كأنّه هو الذي حفرها
لا يساوم
لا يلقي بالاً لشفقة أو وجع لحظيّ
دمٌّ
أحمر قانٍ
يشقّ روحي نصفين
يلخبط أوراقي
وتعاملاتي مع الآخرين
يكتفي ببصمة هادرة
يروق لي أحيانًا أن أضع إصبعي
في ذلك الشق الصغير
كي أوقف التدفق
أو ربما لأعرف كيف يأتي ومن أين!
لونه الأحمر القاني
ألمه الذي لا تحتويه روحي ولا ينقذها منه سوى المخدر
أضع إصبعي بكل بساطة وهدوء
أترك النهر يجري بينهما
دافئًا، متدفقًا، قاتمًا
مشبعًا بالشهوة الضائعة
رائحته تشبه غسيل امرأة ريفية
بالزهرة الزرقاء ورائحة الكلور التي تخترق الأنف
تتسلّل إلى الجسد كلّه
تمنحه رحيقًا لا يماثله شيء

٣٤

تأتي هكذا
رائح تعلق بالروح وتغلقها
تراها واضحة على المعالم
زكية، مختلفة، منادية
كذئبة جائعة بانتظار فريستها
رائحة لا تحمل أسماء كثيرة
تخرق الروح
تحمل الجسد إلى الرغبة
التي تأكل الأخضر واليابس
والجنين في مهده الأول
يأتي الدم هكذا
بلون يحيّر الرسامين في تركيبه
بملامح تتشكّل على الوجه وفي الجسد
لا يدركها إلا خبير..
دم ينتظر كل قمر صيحة الذنب لإعلان وجوده
لا يتشابه وقعه
مرة يأتي سخياً دافقاً متوغلاً
لا يترك مساحة للتنفس أو للنظر
مرة يأتي داكنًا بنيًا يتسلل بصعوبة ولزوجة وغلاظة
ومرة يشفق على ذلك الجسد الهشّ فيأتي هكذا
بوجع خفيفٍ في الرّوح
يكاد لا يجد مكانًا
ينصب رايته بكلّ وقاحة خارجًا للحياة

أشرف فياض

الرائحة الكريهة

تكون الكتابة مثل الهضم في أوقات كثيرة ..
نصاب أحياناً بالإمساك ..
وأحيانٌ أخرى بالإسهال ..
غير أن الأخير قد ينتج نصوصاً رديئة !!
شعور مريح أن تخرج ما في جوفك .. على الأقل أمعائك الغليظة ..
ليس للغرور أو عدمه أي علاقة بالأمر .
أقصد الرائحة الكريهة .
لن أستطيع الحديث عن الحب الآن ..
ليس ثمة علاقة بين الحب والرائحة الكريهة .
هل عدم إدراكنا للرائحة يعد إعاقة ؟
لا أستطيع احترام البشر كثيراً..
جسد المرأة جميل .. مهما حاولوا إخفاءه ..
وتحديد من يستطيع الاستمتاع به ..
الاستمتاع عيب نخفيه ..
والتعصب شرف ..
ندعيه .
القتل مصدر فخر في كثير من الأحيان !
لدرجة أننا قد نُمنح أوسمة ومكافآت وألقاب ..
بل يصل الأمر إلى أن نحكم العالم لأننا قتلنا عدداً كبيراً من البشر!
الجميع متأكدون أنهم على حق .
لماذا بعد هذا كله أفصل بين الحب والرائحة الكريهة ؟!
ولماذا لا أشتاق إليك رغم وجودي وسط غابة من الروائح الكريهة ؟!
ربما هي الرغبة في اشتمام رائحة أخرى ..
لدرجة أنني أدفع المال مقابل ذلك .
الحرب لائقة بالرائحة الكريهة أكثر..
ولدرجة الارتباط !

إسمي يزداد غرابة ..
أتفهمين ما أقصد ؟!

أحياناً أكتب بخط جميل .. أحياناً أكتب بخط رديء ..
أحياناً أحبكِ ..
وأحيانٌ أخرى ..
أحبك !
أقصد حين أكون غاضباً .. منكِ.
لا شيء آخر يستحق أن أغضب لأجله ..
لست غاضباً منك تحديداً ..
بل من تصرفاتك ..
وتعرفين أنني لا أريدك أن تغيري أي شيء فيكِ
لأنني أحببتك هكذا ..
ومستعد للغضب إلى أقصى الحدود ..
وسأبقى أحبك ..
وستبقين تحبين غضبي من تصرفاتك .
الحلقة لا تنتهي .. مثل الكون ..
مثل دوران الكواكب حول شموسها المزاجية ..
ومثل ابتسامتك آخر مرة !!

تشققات جلدية

وطني مر من هنا
منتعلاً حذاء الحرية ..
ثم مضى بعيداً .. تاركاً الحذاء وراءه !
كان يركض بإيقاع مضطرب .. مثل إيقاع قلبي!
قلبي الذي كان يركض باتجاه آخر .. دون مبررٍ مقنع !
حذاء الحرية كان مهترئاً ، بالياً ، ومزيفاً !
مثل باقي القيم البشرية بمختلف مقاساتها .
كل شيء تركني خلفه ومضى .. بما في ذلك أنتِ.
الحذاء اختراعٌ محير ..
يثبت عدم أهليتنا للعيش على هذا الكوكب !
يثبت انتماءنا لمكان آخر لا نحتاج فيه للمشي كثيراً.
أو أن أرضيته مفروشة بالسيراميك الرخيص .. الزلق !!
ليست المشكلة في الانزلاق .. بقدر ما هي مشكلة الماء ..
ومشكلة الحرارة .. والزجاج المكسور .. والأشواك .. والأغصان المتيبسة ..
والصخور المدببة !
الحذاء ليس حلاً مثالياً ..
لكنه يؤدي الغرض المنشود بطريقة ما
تماماً مثل العقل ..
ومثل العاطفة
عاطفتي انطفأت منذ رحلتِ آخر مرة .. ولم أعد قادراً على الوصول إليك ..
منذ احتجازي داخل صندوق إسمنتي مطعم بالقضبان المعدنية الباردة ..
منذ نسيني الجميع بدءاً من حريتي وانتهاءً بحذائي المصاب بأزمة في الهوية!

أوفلاين

هل انتهينا !؟
لم أعد استطيع إرسال هكذا رسالة !
هل لاحظت الفرق ؟
وهل تعتقدين أنها نتيجة طبيعية ؟
ليست طبيعية إلى هذا الحد ، فقد كان من المفترض أن يحصل هذا منذ زمن أبعد
.. أبعد بكثير .. بكثير جداً !
سوف تتسلحين بالصمت كما اعتدت أن تفعلي ، وبانشغالك في قراءة كافكا ،
وربما التعريج على سارتر !
تباً لكل من كافكا وسارتر .. وامرئ القيس !
رغم أن تساؤلات الأخير لم تطرح للمناقشة بشكل جدي ، ربما لأنه كان مدمناً
على الكحول .. أو ربما لأن ليله الطويل ، لم ينته بعد .
خاصة وأن الصباح بالنسبة لي أيضاً .. لا يستحق المراهنة عليه !
نعم سأشتاق إلى مزاجك السيء !
وسأفتقدك بالكامل !
كل مافي الأمر أن عقلي يجبرني على التزام الحياد تجاه مشاعري نحوك ،
وتجاوزها لكي أحافظ على توازناتي الرثة !
لم أعد مهتماً لأمر التوازنات .. فأنا مشتاق جداً لرؤيتك تنظرين بعيداً , حتى وإن
كان كل شيء قريب منك !
هذا ما يفعله عقلي ايضاً !
هو يشبهك لهذه الدرجة !

ملاحظة:

لن أستخدم قلبي في التعبير عن الحب بعد الآن .. فهو متعب لدرجة تفرغه لضخ
الدم فقط ، على اعتبار أنه الخيار الوحيد امامه للتخلص من سطوة الدماغ .
فكلاهما قوة عظمى !!
لا يستطيع أحدهما التخلص من الآخر ، لأنه لا يستطيع البقاء بدونه !
أيهما تختارين أن تكوني ؟
عفواً ، هذا مجرد سؤال افتراضي كنت لأوجهه إليك بشكل مباشر .. في وقت
سابق !
لكن .. ليس بعد الآن !

جلطة دماغية

أعيش أوقاتاً صعبة
والنوم يتصرف كمراهقة وقعت في الحب حديثاً
لن أتطرق لحالة قلبي
ولا إلى الإضطرابات النفسية التي تشبه فقاقيع ماء تجاوزت درجة الغليان
أنا جزء من الكون ..غضب عليه الكون
أنا جزء من الأرض شعرت تجاهه الأرض بالحرج الشديد
أنا بشري بائس
عجز البشر الآخرون عن التزام الحياد معه
الحياد وهم
مثل كل الفضائل التي يتحدث عنها البشر بشكل نظري بالغ الوقاحة
الحق تعريف ناقص مثل الإنسان تماماً
والحب يتنقل كذبابة بائسة
احتجزت داخل مكعب زجاجي
الحرية أمر نسبي جدا
فنحن نعيش في النهاية داخل سجن كروي الشكل
قضبانه من الأوزون
وعندما نتحرر منه يكون مصيرنا الموت المحتوم
أعجز عن الضحك
أعجز تماماً حتى عن الابتسام
أعجز في نفس الوقت حتى عن البكاء
أعجز عن التصرف كبشري ولايحزنني ذلك على الإطلاق
لكنه يؤلمني كثيراً
أن يكون لديك جسد مغطى بشعر خفيف
وأن تمشي على قائمتين
أن تعتمد كلية على عقلك
وأن تنقاد وراء شهوتك لأقصى حد
أن تحتجز حريتك
وأن يقرر الآخرون قتلك
أن تفتقد البشر الأكثر قرباً لك
دون أن تسنح لك فرصة وداعهم
مافائدة الوداع ؟
غير أن تترك انطباعاً حزيناً

٤٠

مافائدة اللقاء ؟

مافائدة الحب ؟

مافائدة أن تكون حياً إلى هذا الحد

في حين يموت الآخرون حزناً عليك

رأيت أبي آخر مرة خلف زجاج سميك

ثم رحل دون رجعة

لنقل بسببي

لنقل أنه لم يحتمل فكرة أن أموت قبله

مات أبي وترك الموت يحاصرني

دون أن أخاف منه بالشكل الكافي

لماذا يرعبنا الموت لدرجة الموت ؟!

رحل أبي بعد أن قضى زمناً طويلاً

على سطح هذا الكوكب

لم أودعه بشكل لائق

لم أحزن عليه بشكل لائق

وعجزت عن البكاء

كعادتي التي تزداد قبحاً مع مرور الوقت

العسكر يحاصرونني من كل إتجاه

ببزاتهم ذات اللون الفقير

تحاصرني القوانين والأنظمة والتشريعات

تحاصرني السيادة

التي لاتستطيع الكائنات الحية التخلص من غريزتها عالية التركيز

تحاصرني وحدتي

تخلقني وحدتي

يختفي الاكتئاب والتوتر والقلق ويقتلني الندم على انتمائي للبشر

عجزت عن توديع كل من أحببتهم ورحلوا ولو بشكل مؤقت

عجزت عن ترك انطباع طيب عن آخر لقاء

ثم استسلمت لبنادق الشوق المصوبة نحوي

رفضت رفع يدي وعجزت عن التحرك

ثم كبلني الحزن ولم يفلح في اجباري على البكاء

الوعي ينهشني من الداخل

ويقضي على كل فرصي بالنجاة

الوعي يقتلني ببطء

والوقت تأخر كثيراً للشفاء منه

مصطفى أبو سنينة

أيُّها الإمبراطور

ليسَ صحيحاً أيُّها الإمبراطور أن "ما لا ينفعُ السربَ،
لا ينفعُ النحلةَ"
اسمح لنحلةٍ مثلي، أن تُصححَ تأمُّلاتكَ بهذا الخبر:
ما عاد هنالكَ من سربٍ لأطيرَ فيهِ
ولا من أزهارٍ بريّة لتفهم لغتي.

الخليّةُ سُحقت تحت بساطيرِ البرابرة.
خانَها من خانْ،
ولو كنتُ أحفظُ صلاةً لرتّلتها على روحِها الباسلة.

زمنُ النحلِ ولَّى أيُّها الإمبراطور
دعني أطيرُ بأجنحتي المتقصّفةِ إلى هاويةٍ أُخرى
فأنا لا عَسلاً ولا شَمعاً تركتُ ورائي
وكلُّ وردةٍ حطَطتُ عليها رطنَتْ بلغةِ البرابرة.

دعني من تأمُّلاتكَ فأنا لن أنفعَ أحداً،
وسيّان إنْ عادَ السربُ أو ما عاد
سيّان أيُّها الإمبراطور.

من كتاب التأمّلات للإمبراطور الروماني ماركوس أورليوس Marcus Aurelius (١٢١-١٨٠).

قشّة

أنا القشّةُ التي تعلّق بها الغريقُ
أعترفُ بجُرمي في غرق أبنائكم في المستنقع.
طوالَ سنواتٍ كنتُ متحفزاً لإسعافِ من يغرقُ
وليسَ من أحدٍ يغرق.
كنتُ أصارعُ التيّارَ المتوحشَ؛ وأرفضُ كلَّ يدٍ تَمتدُّ من اليابسةِ
وأتجذّرُ في المستنقع.
حَسبوني جِذعاً مقطوعاً
حَسبوني حطبةً يابسةً تستعطفُ نارَكم الآفلة،
وحينما سَبحوا لاقتلاعي ممّا سَمَّيْتموهُ بالمستنقع
رُحتُ أراقبُ تقدُّمهم البليدَ
بعَينيْ تِمساح.

٤٣

الزّنْزانة رقم ٨

وَحْدهُ أبي يعلمُ
أيّةَ أخبارٍ سَمعَها من هذا الترانزستور الصغير.
وَحدهُ وبِضعةُ رفاقٍ آخرون.
فأنا لم أكُنْ في سجنِ الرملة لأشهدَ على ذلك.
لا أحدَ كانَ هناك
سوى أبي ورفاقٍ آخرين.
وليسَ أمامي إلا أن أخمّنَ الأخبارَ التي سَمِعها:
الانسحابَ من بيروت
كلمةَ السادات في الكنيست
"الرد في الزمانِ والمكانِ المناسِبيْن"
قصفَ مُفاعلِ تمّوز
وهذا وذاك "خَطٌّ أحمر".
ليسَ أمامي إلا أن أراهُمْ في الزّنْزانة رقم ثمانية
وهم يُحاولُون قتلَ الوقتِ بترانزستورٍ أصْفر.
أنْ أرى الأيام تسيلُ من ظهرِ السنين
وأبي يحفرُ على ظهر الترانزستور
رقمَ الأسر.

وحدَهُ أبي يعلمُ اللعناتِ التي كِيْلت لهذا الترانزستور الأصفر.
وحدهُ يعلمُ الليلَ والقمر، والنهارَ والشمس،
وعددَ النجوم وشكلَ الغيوم
في سجنِ الرملة.
فأنا لمْ أَكُنْ هناكَ لأشهَدَ.
لا أحدَ كانَ هُناك
سوى أبي ورفاق آخرين.
وليسَ أمامي إلا أَنْ أراهُم في الزنزانة رقم ثمانية
وهُم يوقِظونَ الصَّبَاح
ويسقونَ السماءَ ماءً من حَنَفيَّةِ السّجن.
أن أرى صخرةَ الانتصَار التي حمَلوها على ظهورهم
عاماً بعدَ عام
وهُم يستمعونَ إلى أخبارِ الهزائِم.

في شارعِ نابلس

كان اعترافاً بلا كلماتٍ.
أتذكّرُ الشمسَ تغرقُ في ظُلمةِ المستوطنة،
والجنودَ بالبنادقِ يضربونَ الغروبَ
حتى يُغمَى عليه.

صَبٌّ يسرقُ القصائدَ من نزار قباني
ورسائلَ الحب من "الثلجِ (الذي) يأتي من النافذة"
وما زلتُ صَبّاً
رُغمَ أنَّ الشمسَ غرقَتْ في المستوطنة
رغمَ أنَّ اعترافي بالحُبِّ لأوّلِ مرّةٍ
كانَتْ تُهدّدهُ بنادقُ الاحتلال.

عنوان رواية للروائي السوري حنا مينه.

نملة

تحضرُ قصّتي إذا حضَرت قصّةُ الحرب
فلا أحدَ يكترثُ بنملةٍ شجاعةٍ إلا حين يتأمَّلُها قائدٌ مهزوم.

إنّني أسقطُ وأسقطُ وأنهضُ، كُلّما روى جنديٌّ قصّتي.
يقولونَ إنّ لغةَ الحرب تخرجُ من مخازنِ الأسلحة،
لكنّي لا أعرفُ إلا لغةَ القمح
تلك التي أحمِلها منذ سنواتٍ لكي أسقُطَ.

ليتأمَّلني القائدُ كُلّما شَاء
يوماً ما سيأتي من يروي قصّتي التي أعرفها:
عن قائدٍ مهزومٍ تتأمَّلهُ نملةٌ شجاعة.

فريد سليم البيطار

أريحا

أسوق نحو الأسفل
باتجاه غور الأردن
جبالٌ قديمةٌ جدا
الباديةُ ما زالت تقطنُ بها
خطى فيها الرسل
ابراهيم و موسى ومحمد

أوطأ نقطة في الأرض
إلى أين ستذهب سوى للأعلى
مدينة طفولتي
وصلت إلى الحجر المشهور، مستوى سطح البحر
وقفت لأقبله
شعورٌ غريب
أذني غُلِقتْ من الضغط
وزوجتي ما عادت تسمع
وصلتُ إلى حدود المدينة
الحراس، الجيش الإسرائيلي
بدأت الأسئلة
لقد مُنِعتُ دخول مدينتي عشرين عاماً
ولكن ليس هذه المره
الله كبير
بعدها وصلتُ إلى الحارس الفلسطيني
أراضي فلسطين المحررة
قلت السلام عليكم
قال وعليكم السلام

مرحباً بك يا بني
الحراس يتبسمون
وأنا كذلك مبتسمٌ

مررتُ على مستشفى الرأس
تعرف، هربتُ من بيتي
في سن الرابعة
لأبحث عن والدي
الذي لا يمكثُ في البيت أبداً
أُماه قالت
أبوك ملك التفاح في الشغل
قُلتُ في رأسي
أنا أعرف السوق
ضربتني سياره الدجاج
أمام المستشفى بالضبط
حملوني إليها ورأسي مكسور

بحثت عن البيت الذي رُبيتُ فيه
ما زال موجود
قلت مرحباً للشُرْفه
التي كنت أنامُ فيها في أيام الحر في الصيف
نفس الشُرْفه التي رأيتُ
منها شهداء الحرب
عندما هجمَ العدو على مدينتي النائمه

رشفت شاي النعنع
أريحا عندها أجود شاي نعنع في الأرض
ذقت برتقال أريحا العذب
شعرتُ بأنني عدتُ إلى طفولتي السعيده
عندما كُنتُ أشمُ رائحة المطر
الذي يتبخّر في أيام الصيف
يذهب في ثواني
عندما كُنتُ أمشي وراء أخي
ذاهبٌ إلى المدرسة، تراسنطه

أريحا أريحا
بيت جبل قرنطل، جبل المسيح
وقصور الأمويين
وبيت أحلى أشجار الليمون
عندما كنت أشمُ رائحة الياسمين تملؤ الشوارع

ولكن أيضاً
بيت مخيمات اللاجئين
بيت الفقر والجحيمُ والمهانة في هذه الأيام

سُقتُ في الغور بجانب نهر الأردن
حيث غَسل المسيح أرجله
سُقتُ إلى بحيرة طبريا إلى الناصره
بلدة رسولٌ مشهور

أريحا أريحا
بيت البحر الميت
حيثُ لا يعيشُ شيٌ فيه
حتى الأسماكُ غادرت

٢٠٠٦/١١/٢٧

ترجمة فريد سليم محمود البيطار

النكبة

النكبة والنكسة
لقد رويت هذه القصة
مئات المرات
بحيث انني بدات انسى
كيف كانت البداية
في حياة بلا نهاية
والدتي روت منتصف الحكاية
والدي امتنع عن الكلام
دائما اتحدث عن الماضي
حيثما يجب ان ابني المستقبل
المشكلة في الموضوع
كلما ابني العش
صهيون يهدمه
البداية كانت بسيطه
طفل بريء
تربى في قرية نائمه
أريحا
ما زلت اتذكر شاي النعناع
ما زلت اشم رائحة المطر المتبخر

ترجمة فريد سليم محمود البيطار

ما بقيت إلا الحجارة

مرة أخرى وأخرى
الحجارة تسقط على رأسي
والاموات كثيرون
لتلومهم
ما بقيت إلا الحجارة

أم أحمد تندب على حالها
حاملةٌ حجر في يدها اليمنى
وتلطخُ وجهها في اليد الأخرى
تصرخ وتقول:

"أين هو بيتي الجميل
أين هي حياتي
أين ابني الذي أفتشُ عليه

أنا حاملةٌ لعبته المفضلة
لقد وجدت يداهُ
لقد وجدتُ قدماهُ
ولكن لا أجدُ رأسهُ"

تَسألُ مرةً أخرى:
"أين ابني الجميل أحمد
أين زوجي الغالي
أين بيتي الذي تهدّم"

أنا لا أتحدثُ عن
الرؤوس المتكلمة

"ما بقيت إلا الحجارة
مرى أخرى وأخرى
تسقطُ على رأسي

أنا سأبني الشجاعية
أنا سأبني كل حجرٍ هُدم
أنا سأبني بيتٌ حانونٌ"

الذي قصفه الشيطان الصهيوني

والأموات الشهداء بالآف كثيرون

لنتهمهم بالمجزرة

ما بقيت إلا الحجارة

٢٠١٤/٨/٢٧، خلال غزو ال٥٢ يوما على غزة والذي راح ضحيته ٢١٨٥
شهيد

ترجمة فريد سليم محمود البيطار الشاعر الإنسان

الألم الذي لا يشفى

تحدث إلى الطيور عن ذلك
قالوا لي "افعل ما نقوم به دائما
تطير إلى مكان آخر
ثم يعود مع بداية جديدة
إلى نفس المكان الذي بدأت"

وشجرة الزيتون تستمع
أخبرتني "سوني لا تستمع إلى الطيور
أنظر الي، أنا في نفس المكان منذ عصور
يقتلعوني، ليتمكن جنود جيش "الدفاع" الإسرائيلي من الحصول على رؤية أفضل
أنا أطفو على السطح دائما
نجوت الإمبراطوريات
وذهبوا، وأنا ما زلت هنا ".

كان يستمع إلىTillis Darby
ويخرج ما عنده
عن ألمه الذي لا يشفي-٢٠ سنوات حتى الآن
أمضى ٨ سنوات في انتظار تنفيذ حكم الإعدام في سجون شيكاغو
لجريمة لم يرتكبها
قدمت الشرطة لائحة التهم
برأ الآن
يبكي حتى الآن عن ألمه

تفتح جروحي
في كل مرة يغزو الإسرائيليين غزة
والأساطيل التي لا تصل أبدا
شعبي الذي يعيش على دولار واحد في اليوم
ألمي لا يزول.

ترجمة فريد سليم محمود البيطار

نعومي شهاب ناي

كل شيء في عالمنا لا يبدو مناسباً

ذات مرة بدأوا بغزونا
بسلب بيوتنا وأشجارنا ورسِم الخرائط
وألقونا الى أماكن ضيّقة.
لم تكن تلك مساومة أو صفقة ولا حتى حرباً حقيقية.
إلى يومنا هذا يزعمون بأنها كانت كذلك
لكنها كانت شيئا آخر.
تأسّفنا على ما حدث لهم
ولكن لم يكن لدينا أي علاقة معه.
لا تفكر أنت في قطعة أرض صغيرة
إلا حين يسلبها منك أحدهم،
ولا يمكنك العودة إليها.
قدماك تريدان المشي هناك.
إنك تسقط الآن مثل غبار شريدٍ،
مثل شعور بالضياع.
أبكي وأنا أتذكر بممر بيتنا
والحجر البارد في الباب.
مرت سنوات ولا شيء يناسب بشكل صحيح.
أتوا بالبنادق والوعود والزي العسكري.
قالت مجلة "لايف":
"كن من المستغرب أن يعثر على بعض العرب
ما زالوا يسكنون في منازلهم".
من المستغرب؟ وبأي مكان آخر يمكننا أن نكون؟
فوق التلال؟
نتحدث مع النعناع والخراف، ونحنج نحفر بالتراب؟

لِماذا كانت حاجة شخص آخر الى بيت
أهم من حاجتنا الى بيوتنا وقد عشنا فيه؟
لم يستطيع أحد أن يشرح هذا بشكل كافي.
لكنهم يجدون أشياء أُخرى ويثرثرون عنها.

ترجمة وليد البزون وجوش كلفو

عطشان

"قتل الاسرائيليون صبيا فلسطينيا في المظاهرة..."

كل يوم تتحدث الأخبار عن "المناضل" –
قد يكون على الأرجح صبياً
ذو قلب كسير، يقوم بشيء يائس
وانا اشتقت لك. لقد عرفت.
عرفت أن أحمد موسى غادر مبكرا.
متظاهرا ضد الجدار الذي فصل أشجار زيتون قريته
عن الناس الذين يعتنون بها، وينقلون منها دلاء الماء.
الناس المجتمعين المغنيين اغنية الزيتون
طوال أيامهم.
لا تذهب هناك، رجته عائلته.
ابن عشرة أعوام يدافع عن الأشجار.
لكن من غيره يصبر؟
رصاصة في جبين أحمد موسى.
"اجتمع المعزون حول أب الصبي
الذي اتكأ على جدار".
جدار المشرحة هذه المرة.
حافظ عليها يا أبي.
حيثما أنت، حافظ عليها
على الأشجار التي لا تعرف أين غادر أهلها
ومتى يعودون.

ترجمة وليد البزون وجوش كلفو

أمير وأنّا

شيء لا يصدق، دوامة العنف هذه، وكيف لا يدرك أي من الطرفين بأنهما خاسران
د. كايرو عرفات، الضفة الغربية

أمير لا ينام.
يختبئ تحت السرير.
أنّا خائفة من كل شيء.
من السيارات الواقفة ومن الباصات المتحركة.
أنّا خائفة من الخبز المُحمّص.
اسماهما يبدآن بحرف الألف،
ويحتويان على عدد الحروف ذاتها.
ويعيشان على بعد ميل واحد.
لم يهبهما أحد
ما يستحقانه.
حول منزليهما
حول كل البيوت العربية واليهودية،
تنام شقائق النعمان
تحت الحصى والأوساخ.
وماذا تدري؟
في آذار تنمو العيدان الخضراء
رؤوسها ترفرف
صاعدةً في كل اتجاه.

ترجمة لأحمد طه عبد ربه مع رفاييل كوهين

الحكي للأبد
(لفلسطين ودارين طاطور)

قلها مرّة أخرى: قاومُ عشر مرّات

الذين ليسوا سياسيين
الذين يذهبون إلى المدرسة أو يعانون بالغرف
والدكاكين والمكتبات والمطابخ وأغصان النعناع المتدلية من علبة
ويغيرون الحفاظات ويمسحون اللعاب من على الذقون
ويخرطون البصل ويقطعون الخيار من الكرمة الشائكة،
كنّا نودّ فعل أي شيء لك يا فلسطين.
لكن كل ما عرفنا ان نقوم به هو الكلام.
الكلام لكل من اتفق معنا مسبقًا.
نوقّع الالتماسات ونتّصل بالنوّاب ونكتب الشيكات،
ونرتدي الكوفيات المربوطة على أعناقنا ونتظاهر
ونأمل أن يقف الرئيس أوباما (بعبقريته العظيمة)
معكم حقا. هل كان يمكننا فعل شيء آخر؟
مخاطبة أولئك الذين لم يتفقوا معنا؟ لكن من نحن؟
"لو عرفوا قصصنا لما فعلوا هذه الأشياء بنا"،
قالت جدّتي الفلسطينية عندما بلغت المائة
بعد أن سالت دموعها بسبب الغاز الإسرائيلي في غرفتها.
لم تكن غاضبة هي، بل نحن.
دارين محاصرة في بيتها لاستخدامها كلمة " قاومُ" ― هي كانت هناك
وكنا نحن في كل مكان آخر. معاقبتُها أمرٌ سهلٌ
فليس لإسرائيل مشكلة في الحصار والظلم والقمع والتلاعب في الأسماء.
أمّا المضغوطون لزمن طويل بلا نفوذ على الأسلحة أو الحدود،
فمن السهل تجاهلهم ونكرانهم ولومهم،
اللوم دائماً، وتغيير القصة وقلب الحقائق وهم بالتأكيد، يا ستّي، عارفون القصة
لأنّ الجميع حكاها، دارين حكتها،
ومحمود وفدوى وإدوارد وسهير وانطون وشريف ونتالي وليزا ولينا
وخالد وسلمى ورجاء وفادي وعزيز، كلهم حكوها واستمرّوا يحكونها.
الحكي للأبد. ولكن طالت الطوابير أمام الحواجز وازدحمت

وصغرت البساتين الحزينة، ولاح الجدار في الأفق مخاطا بمزيد من الصرخات كما ينمو كابوس بدوامات الممرات والمتاريس والأبواب المغلقة والزنازين والأقوياء يستمرون بالقول: أعطوا الظالمين مزيداً من المال إنهم الديمقراطية. والنائم يصرخ من الكابوس: استيقظ!
فقط دعني أستيقظ.

ترجمة لأحمد طه عبد ربه مع رفاييل كوهين

فادي جودة

محاكاة

لم تُرد ابنتي
أن تُؤذ عنكبوتا
كان يُعششُ بين مقبضي دراجتِها
انتظرت أسبوعين
حتى ذهب بمشيئته

قلتُ لها: إن مزَّقتِ نسيجَهُ
سيعلم أن منزله ليس هنا
و سيمكنُكِ التنزه بدراجتك

قالت: أما كذلك يُصبِحُ
آخرون لاجئين؟

ترجمة فادي جودة

في النهر مرّتان

بعد دراسة أوجهنا لأشهر
أدرك ابني أن الإشراق مهمته

سيقضي سنوات بفك طلاسم الحبِ
ظلمهِ وأوهامه
فهو لم يأتِ لهذا العالم بإرادته،
وكل إرادةٍ استدراك

ماذا سأخبره عن الأرض
واللغة ومقابر تسكن صمت أبي،
لعل أمي تعرف:

في الفيلم، لا يستطيع المسلوبون العودة
ولا حتى أمواتا -
توبيخ ما مس الإعلامي
الذي لم يظن الأمر مهماً أو ظنه مبالغة

هل سأقول لابني أن كل الأمم
تنشأ بعد قتلٍ جماعي، وأني لا أحفظ

نشيداً وطنياً عن ظهر قلب
ولا حتى أغنية عن "البيسبول"؟

عليّ أن انتبه للزهور والغيوم،
حكمة قديمة قيلت مرارا وجيدا
وها قد حط الليل

وابني يحدّق
في عيني أمه من حوض الاستحمام،
"قيس وليلي" تقول بعد يوم عملٍ طويل

وحين يقهقه يهز أكتافه بلا وعي
ينصب نسيجا
في نواةٍ ما بدماغه يعتقد العلم
أنها مثوى الحب

أحتى الحب مكان؟ يا ابني
لا تحب بلداً ولا تكره آخر
وتذكّر الجرائم أحيانا

تخلّد ضحاياها
وأحيانا تخلّد الجلاد

أتتذكُر تحديقك في رعشة
الأوراق على فروعها؟

ولا تصدق صوت البحر
في صَدفة، صدّق البحر
ذاك المجاز الذي لا ينتهي

ولا تقُل الكثير عن لغة غيرك
تعَلم أن تحبها
بصمت من يرعى من يموت فيها
ومن يحيى

ترجمة فادي جودة

إنتقام

الإنتقام ليس ما تريد بل تريد
ما لا يمكنك تسميته وهو يُسميك

الإنتقام على خطاك
فلتكن، بعدك، الكلمات

لي جسداً
تلعق أذنيّ ضد الإنتقام

مساومة الأصالة

أحبك أكثر مما يحب العالم ذاته
العالم لا يحب ذاته كثيرا

تشابه أبديّ
مقسوم على ما هو عابر

حمار وحشي
في علم الجبر

ترجمة فادي جودة

ديمة ك. شهابي

نطاق المصادرة

ممسحة أرجل متربة،
نفس يتلاشى في الفم،
تاريخ ممزّق في جسد
عصفور مهشّم على حاجز الشباك.
لحم طريدة منبسط في طبق مع الفطر
في منتجع بحيرة سميت باسم قبيلة منقرضة.
بيت دمشقي قديم مع أفاعي صغيرة
في ثقوب جدرانه الباردة.
لطخة صدئة على وجه امرأة
تضاء بوهج المراقبة في الظلام.
طفل لديه حلم واضح
حيث يركض ويقفز على أشجار السنط في الساحل.
نباتات الدفلى شبه مبرهمة مقصوصة الى أنصاف
في منتصف أيلول.
بيت مهجور مشبع بزهور الخردل الصفراء
حيث كشط شخص الضوء به
منتصفَ الليل وأرعب الأطفال.
طفل في العاشرة وبيده M١٦ في تيباني
وهو يفضّل الذهاب إلى المدرسة.
حوار مع حبيبي حيث يقول:
لماذا النحيب على منظر أيد صغيرة ممدودة؟
غدا نذهب باتجاه الجنوب.

ترجمة لأحمد طه عبد ربه مع رفاييل كوهين

غزة رنغا

من الجانب السفلي
للسعفة حين يلتحم
البحر بالأرض، إحدى

امرأة تشمّس ذراعها،
أطراف أحدهم مطوية في شفاه

فستانها الطويل المطرّز بالحور
تقول "رأيت دخانا".
"لم يكن دخانَ

أرض جرداء ولا
نزيفَ أطفال يتامى"

***

الأرض هي كل ما نحزن
لأجله... بأحلام ضبابية

في الساعات الملبدة بالدخان
انسدَّ ضوء النهار من عيوننا

ولا شيء مرسوم أبدا:
والرضيع فوق

جثة الأم اليابسة
في وضح النهار

***

أثر الحذاء الملطخ بالزيت
على الحجاب
وعلى الجدار أيضا

وما زالت رائحة الغاز
تضمخ ملابس الفتاة

وأُخرى ذات صوت متألم
تصرخ... لماذا، لمن؟
الشرفات، البنايات،

وسيارة إسعاف بلا سائق
تظل في سقف حلقها.

ترجمة لأحمد طه عبد ربه مع رفاييل كوهين

أنت منها، أكثر أو أقل للأبد

قلت للصبي
الذي سأل لماذا هجر ابراهيم هاجر في الصحراء.
وللاجابة يجب ان تحدق بسخرية الحب
ولا يجب ان تطيح بها شجرة المغنولية،
طازجة جدا وقريبة بصورة خطرة
وخيط رفيع من العفن البني يطوق
ازهار زهرية بيضاء كبيرة في بداية الربيع،
ليس لتقشير عيون الصبي
من الخيانات الاولى
وقبائل التاريخ المقيدة والمكسرة،
او من النساء اللواتي يتوسلن بالله من اجل الماء في الصحراء.
ومن سيخبر عن مستقبل الصبي
الذي تصاعد على هذا الرصيف
الذي تناثرت به بتلات مسحوقة
او ربما سيجد جوابا
من نافورة مشفرة
ويدعوها زمزم او حب
خال من السخرية،
او علامة ضد الحب
تغرق في العطش،
او إذا تتسأل لماذا
ادارت امه ظهرها لسؤاله
وسوف تتسأل هي
ماذا سيسمي رفضها عن الاجابة.

ترجمة وليد البزون وجوش كلفو

عنوان هذه القصيدة مأخوذة من مقال إدوارد سعيد المهم *تأملات في المنفى*

محمود درويش

ذباب أخضر

المشهد هو هو. صيف وعرق. وخيال يعجز عن رؤية ما وراء الأفق. واليوم أفضل من الغد. لكّن القتلى هوم الذين يتجدّدون. يولدون كل يوم. وحين يحاولون النوم يأخذهم القتل من نعاسهم الى نوم بلا أحلام. لا قيمة للعدد. ولا أحد منهم يطلب عونا من أحد. أصوات تبحث عن كلمات في البرية، فيعود الصدى واضحا جارحا: لا أحد. ولكّن ثمة من يقول: "من حقّ القاتل أن يدافع عن غريزة القتل." أمّا القتلى فيقولون متأخرين: "من حقّ الضحية أن تدافع عن حقّها في الصراخ." يعلو الأذان صاعدا من وقت الصلاة الى جنازات متشابهة. توابيت مرفوعة على عجل، تدفن على عجل... اذ لا وقت لإكمال الطقوس، فإن قتلى آخرين قادمون، مسرعين، من غارات أخرى. قادمون فرادى أو جماعات... أو عائلة واحدة لا تترك وراءها أيتاما وثكالى. السماء رماديّة رصاصية. والبحر رماديّ أزرق. أمّا لون الدم فقد حجبته عن الكاميرا أسراب من ذباب أخضر!

كقصيدة نثرية

صَيْفٌ خريفيٌّ على التلال كقصيدةٍ نثرية. النسيمُ إيقاعٌ خفيفٌ أُحسَّ به و لا أسمعه في تواضع الشجيرات. والعشب المائل إلى الاصفرار صُوَرٌ تتقشَّف، وتُغْري البلاغةَ بالتشبُّه بأفعالها الماكرة. لا احتفاء على هذه الشعاب إلاّ بالمتاح من نشاط الدُوريِّ، نشاط يراوح بين معنىً وعَبَث. والطبيعة جسد يتخفَّف من البهرجة والزينة، ريثما ينضج التين والعنب والرُمَّان ونسيانُ شهواتٍ يوقظها المطر. "لولا حاجتي الغامضة إلى الشعر لما كُنْتُ في حاجة إلى شيء" يقول الشاعر الذي خفَّتْ حماستُهُ فقلَّتْ أخطاؤه. ويمشي، لأن الأطباء نصحوه بالمشي بلا هدف لتمرين القلب على لامبالاةٍ ما ضروريّةٍ للعافية. وإذا هَجَسَ، فليس بأكثَرَ من خاطرةٍ مجانيّة. الصيف لا يصلح للإنشاد إلاّ فيما ندر. الصيف قصيدةٌ نثرية لا تكترث بالنسور المحلقة في الأعالي.

أبعد من التماهي

أجلِسُ أمام التلفزيون، إذ ليس في وسعي أن أفعل شيئاً آخر. هناك، أمام
التلفزيون، أعثر على عواطفي. وأرى ما يحدث بي ولي. الدخانُ يتصاعد مني،
وأمدُّ يدي المقطوعةَ لأمسك بأعضائي المبعثرة من جسوم عديدة، فلا أجدها ولا
أهرب منها من فرط جاذبيّة الألم. أنا المحاصر من البرّ والجو والبحر واللغة.
أقلعتُ آخرُ طائرةٍ من مطار بيروت، ووَضَعَتْني أمام التلفزيون، لأرى بقيّة موتي
مع ملايين المشاهدين. لا شيء يثبت أني موجود حين أفكّر مع ديكارت، بل حين
ينهض مني القربانُ، الآن، في لبنان. أدخل في التلفزيون، أنا والوحش. أعلم أن
الوحش أقوى مني في صراع الطائرة مع الطائر. ولكني أدْمَنْتُ، ربما أكثر مما
ينبغي، بُطُولَةَ المجاز: التَهَمَني الوحش ولم يهضمني. وخرجتُ سالماً أكثر من
مرة. كانت روحي التي طارت شعاعاً مني ومن بطن الوحش تسكن جسداً آخر
أخفَّ وأقوى. لكني لا أعرف أين أنا الآن: أمام التلفزيون، أم في التلفزيون. أما
القلب فإني أراه يتدحرج، ككوز صنوبر، من جبل لبناني إلى غزة!

نيرون

ماذا يدور في بال نيرون، وهو يتفرّج على حريق لبنان؟ عيناه زائغتان من النشوة، ويمشي كالرقص في حفلة عرس: هذا جنون، جنوني، سيّد الحكمة، فلتشتعلوا النار في كل شيء خارج طاعتي... وعلى الأطفال أن يتأدبوا ويتهذبوا ويكفوا عن الصراخ بحضرة أنغامي!

ماذا يدور في بال نيرون، وهو يتفرّج على حريق العراق؟ يسعده أن يوقظ في تاريخ الغابات ذاكرة تحفظ اسمه عدوا لحمورابي وجلجامش وأبي نواس: شريعتي هي أم الشرائع. وعشبة الخلود تنمو في مزرعتي. والشعر، ما معنى هذه الكلمة؟

ماذا يدور في بال نيرون، وهو يتفرّج على حريق فلسطين؟ يبهجه أن يدرج اسمه في قائمة الأنبياء نبيّا لم يؤمن به أحد من قبل. نبيّا للقتل كلفه الله بتصحيح الأخطاء التي لا حصر لها في الكتب السماوية: "أنا أيضا كليم الله!"

ماذا يدور في بال نيرون، وهو يتفرّج على حريق العالم؟ "أنا صاحب القيامة". ثم يطلب من الكاميرا وقف التصوير، لأنه لا يريد لأحد أن يرى النار المشتعلة في أصابعه في نهاية هذا الفيلم الأمريكي الطويل!

سارة صالح

العود

تخبرني أن العود ليس من شغفك
فاعلم أنني..
قد استنفدت شغفي في إبقائنا
على قيد الأمل
قد سرقوا كل أمانينا..
ومن أوتار عروبتنا
صنعوا المثل..
فليفعلوا ما طاب لهم
فصوت العود يجري
في دمي..
وفي بحري والجبل..
نتقاسم السر معا..
أسمعه ويطربني
ألحانا تؤرقني..
تطارد الموت في شوارعنا
لعله يتركنا ويرتحل..
قوافله تمضي
بين أزقتنا..
فالأمر جلل
فليس أقل من نغمة حزن
نندندنها..
قد باتت أوتار عودي
تعزف ألحانا من وجل

ترجمة وجدان شمالة

المدن التي غيرتنا

دبي ٢٠٠١

ارتفع ثمن كل شيء عدا
أرواح البشر...
فكلما دقت أجراس الجوع
في بُطُون الفقراء...
زادتهم رخصا

بيروت ٢٠٠٥

لم يبق منك سوى قطعة
فلا تحزني!
فالقطعة الناقصة من اللوحة...
تجعلها مشوهة

براغ ٢٠٠٦

صندوق من الجواهر
أضعت مفتاحه...
ولا أملك إلا أن أجثو
أمامه على ركبتي...
بكفين مفتوحتين
تملؤها الأماني ...

القدس ٢٠١٣

إن القليل مما قلت...
قد حطم السفن على مرفئي
فلا تنطق عما تبقى...
فلم يعد هناك
سوى الأشلاء

سيدني ٢٠١٢

قد تبدو
أبوابك مفتوحة
لتقبل الاختلاف...
لكنا في الواقع مغلقة دون
البشر ممن هم على شاكلتي...
أقف في صف طويل
انتظر دوري...
من بين أدوار الباحثين عن ذاتهم
تغيرت ألسنتهم
وما زالت أسماؤهم...
مدفونة في حناجرهم
علي... أحمد... محمد
لا شيء يساوي الشعور
بأنك حر... ولو كنت
في أكوام من الظلام

القاهرة ٢٠١٤

التاريخ يكتبه المنتصر
فإن خشي الافتراء...
اختصر!

نيويورك، ليلة رأس السنه

من بين متاحف الدنيا
التي زرتها...
لم يسعني اكتشاف
مكنونات متحفك أنت
وفيك أقيم ما يعجبني
أن أتيه فيه... الفن والتاريخ

سيدني ٢٠١٥

ترحل أنفاسي إليك
فينتهي عالمي...
ليخلق من جديد!

ترجمة وجدان شمالة